SCHOOL DISCIPLINE

SCHOOL DISCIPLINE
Order and Autonomy

Ellen Jane Hollingsworth
Henry S. Lufler, Jr.
William H. Clune III

PRAEGER SPECIAL STUDIES • PRAEGER SCIENTIFIC

New York • Philadelphia • Eastbourne, UK
Toronto • Hong Kong • Tokyo • Sydney

Library of Congress Cataloging in Publication Data

Hollingsworth, Ellen Jane.
　　School discipline, order and autonomy.

　　Bibliography:　p.
　　Includes index.
　　1.　School discipline—United States.　I. Lufler,
Henry S.　II.　Clune, William H., 1942-　　　III.　Title.
LB3012.H64　1984　　　　　　371.5'0973　　　83-24544
ISbn 0-03-070086-8 (alk. paper)

Published in 1984 by Praeger Publishers
CBS Educational and Professional Publishing
a Division of CBS Inc.
521 Fifth Avenue, New York, NY 10175 USA
© 1984 by Praeger Publishers

456789 052 987654321

Printed in the United States of America
on acid-free paper

To Rogers and Lauren Hollingsworth
--E.J.H.

To my parents, Ruth and Hank Lufler,
for showing that support and love reduce
the need for discipline.
--H.S.L.

To all those hurt by and compensating for
the pressures of work and money on child
rearing, and to Connie, for doing it right.
--W.H.C.

ACKNOWLEDGEMENTS

The school discipline research reported in this book was made possible by three grants from the Wisconsin Council on Criminal Justice using program funds from the Law Enforcement Assistance Administration. Awards totalling $210,000 were made to the Center for Public Representation in Madison, Wisconsin, from 1976 to 1979. The Center, a public interest law firm and research institute, has a staff drawn in part from the University of Wisconsin–Madison Law School faculty and from other schools and colleges on the Madison campus. Our special thanks among Center personnel go to Louise G. Trubek, executive director, and to Karen Allenstein, project secretary and coordinator, for their continuing support and assistance.

The school discipline research project was directed by Henry S. Lufler, Jr., whose earlier work at the Center led to this study; he took the lead in developing the research agenda and data collection instruments. Ellen Jane Hollingsworth, project codirector, focused on data analysis efforts, organizing the mass of empirical and observational data generated in the field. William H. Clune III assisted in the development of the project's theoretical framework and provided general guidance as the project progressed.

The project was staffed by a research team with varied academic backgrounds. Joseph Frees served as Senior Research Associate, was our anthropologist in residence at the schools we studied, and otherwise supervised the on-site observations and managed data-collection logistics. Barry J. Teicher joined the project after the first year and, drawing on his skills as a former Milwaukee high school teacher, served as Field Coordinator, assuming the time-consuming task of helping observe discipline and coordinating the organization of hundreds of pages of field notes.

Two persons who joined the project as student workers, Michael A. Roth and Eric L. Haralson, stayed on to become full-time members of the research team. The project also involved graduate research assistants drawn from the University of Wisconsin–Madison Law School and the Departments of Curriculum and Instruction, Political Science, and Sociology. These were David B. Bills, Christine B. Harrington, Donald A. Hermanson, Geoffrey A. Tabakin, and Simon P. Tonkin.

vi

Project advisors helped to review the progress of the research and, more importantly, made their individual skills available to the researchers. The group included Professor David M. Trubek, U.W. Law School, who coordinated the advisors, working with the project from its inception, and U.W. Professors Michael W. Apple, Department of Curriculum and Instruction, Malcolm M. Feeley, Department of Political Science, Nathan P. Feinsinger, Law School, and the late Eleanor Roe, Law School, and James Scamman, Stevens Point (Wisconsin) Area School District Administrator. Professor Chris Argyris, Harvard University, contributed useful ideas concerning the problems of change in large-scale organizations. Several individuals read and made helpful comments on portions of the manuscript. These included Professor Vandra L. Masemann, University of Toronto; Professor Michael R. Olneck, U.W. Educational Policy Studies Department; Felicity Skidmore, U.W. Institute for Research on Poverty, and Ann K. Wallace, U.W. Education Dean's Office. Helen H. Tetzlaff, Education Dean's Office, suffered through numerous manuscript changes and produced the final version with both skill and good humor.

Our appreciation also goes to the public school personnel in Madison, Wisconsin, who permitted us to pretest survey and interview instruments. Finally, thanks to more than 1,500 students, 230 teachers, and 100 other school personnel who were study participants in "Middle City" and "Rural Place" where the data were collected. Though they remain, by choice, anonymous, they made the research possible.

CONTENTS

LIST OF TABLES

SCHOOL DISCIPLINE

Chapter 1

CONCEPTUALIZING SCHOOL DISCIPLINE

A. The Problem of School Discipline

This book is about discipline in American public schools--an issue which poll after poll indicates to be foremost in people's minds as they think about schools.[1] Discipline is also, for many teachers, the issue that turns enthusiasm into burnout.[2] Not infrequently, discipline (or the lack of discipline) is a subject for Sunday magazine supplement articles.[3] Yet, for all this attention, little systematic research has been conducted about discipline. There are a few books and articles focusing on how the individual teacher can handle discipline more satisfactorily,[4] and there are profiles of alternative programs for discipline.[5] But the literature is sparse, and usually confined to the abstract.

This book presents a sociology of discipline in the school setting, using empirical data and site observation to illuminate the role of discipline. It draws on junior and senior high schools in a middle-sized community school system which we call "Middle City" and a combined junior-senior high school in a small farm community we call "Rural Place." It seeks to find out how discipline is perceived by the different parties in the school, what the daily disciplinary events are, and how discipline-related activities are integrated with the myriad other activities and problems of school life.

Discipline is more than who broke what rule how often and with what punishment. We are concerned with identifying how serious school disorders really are, what aspects of the discipline system are most problematic, and what, if anything, schools might do to achieve a better fit between their need for order and the need for student development of autonomy. The whole world of discipline--the rules, the

1

enforcers, and often the troublemakers--is deeply rooted in the goals and structures of the school. A school often cannot change its pattern of discipline without addressing broad educational issues and the structure of schooling itself.

This book suggests that there are fundamental assumptions and choices about order and autonomy underlying the discipline policies in school. Further, it suggests that, although there is an ultimate trade-off between autonomy and order (the more you have of one, the less you have of the other), most schools have discipline policies which fail to maximize autonomy and order.

Approaches to the Study of Discipline. Discipline in schools is a subject on which educators, parents, and theorists have enormously varied points of view. Often these points of view are not explicitly or clearly articulated, adding to the difficulty of measuring the reality of behavior against some preferred ideal. The divergence among the major ways of looking at discipline accounts for some of the confusion in the school world, in that people involved with defining discipline (and carrying it out) do not agree and are often unaware how their attitudes differ. To put the matter another way, people talking about discipline are not all talking about the same thing. It will be helpful, initially, to sketch the major perspectives from which people view discipline.

There is an influential group of thinkers who focus on discipline as part of the systematic development of maturing youth.[6] To them, discipline in schools is a part of the process by which an individual develops a sense of moral order and orchestrates a sense of responsibility to self with responsibility to family, peer groups, institutions, and general society. Discipline is both a process and a standard, as the maturing child extends his or her capacity for responsibility, ultimately becoming an integrated part of the moral order. The function of a properly conceived discipline system, according to this view, is to promote the capacity of the individual and the institution to act interdependently, with the discipline system exhibiting concern for the balance between individual autonomy and social order, and with the ultimate effect that the individual has an appreciation of the moral order and his/her obligations toward maintaining it. This perspective obviously moves beyond order for the sake of order, linking the context of discipline to individual maturation, which in turn affects the good of society. Discipline, from the moral order point of view, is both individual and institutional, with personal development aggregating into social civility.

Another conceptualization of discipline, much less concerned for the emergence of the responsible individual, emphasizes the organizational context of discipline.[7] Writers with this perspective stress that schools are organizations which are more concerned with maintaining uniformity than with fostering diversity, an emphasis schools have developed in order to achieve the goals society expects of them. However strong the interest of schools in providing maximal learning environments for individual pupils, schools give even more emphasis to minimums, regularity of performance, and technology-oriented batch processing rather than individual or particular achievement. A part of this attention to uniformity, the argument goes, is the considerable emphasis on control of students. Although there are many questions as to how much schools as organizations control teachers, there is very little conceptual disagreement with the conclusion that schools control students (or try to).

Discipline in schools, from this perspective, is an activity or set of activities carried out by the schools as part of their addressing of basic tasks. Discipline is an organizational necessity, and the major characteristics of the discipline system are shaped more by the needs of organizations to function in social environments than by the desire to respond to social and psychological needs of youth. From this view of discipline, it follows that the nature of the school organization--its sharing of authority, the amount of decentralization, the attitude toward outside information--very much shapes the definition and content of discipline. Certain kinds of organizations, the arguments goes, require certain kinds of social control, and it is to organizational variables that one must look, not pupil or staff characteristics or educational theory, to explain discipline.

A third view holds that discipline is part of the teaching of obedience and respect for authority necessary to prevent youths from raising social or economic challenges to the ongoing system.[8] This view derives, often, from the philosophical position that schooling (particularly in capitalist countries) functions as a tool used by the ruling classes to socialize youth into accepting the prevailing economic and social systems as legitimate. The institution of the school, in this view, is to legitimate the social order in the eyes of the young, and discipline is simply an adjunct of the system of socialization. The socializing institution, to serve as an effective mechanism for the transmission of culture, must permit minimum latitude. Thus schooling must be compulsory, at least when industrialization reaches the point where children are no longer needed as workers. The school as an institution must demonstrate its unassailable authority through its ability to discipline miscreants. The system of discipline is deliberately designed to prevent challenge, to promote order and acceptance without question.

So far as rights are discussed in school systems of discipline, they are firmly attached to responsibilities. Like the exponents of the moral order point of view, those who espouse this view of discipline posit strong links between the micro (the individual student) and the macro (society).

The fourth distinctive way of looking at discipline in schools, based on concepts of common law, is <u>in loco parentis</u>.[9] The theory posits that the teacher may be delegated some parental authority (during the school day). Teachers are to maintain discipline in the school, much as the parent does in the home. It is the responsibility of the school--for the sake of the children--to impose and execute systems of discipline. The theory has been expanded on occasion so that schools have assumed authority to protect morals, safety, and welfare of students, as well as to regulate appearance and curricular matters. <u>In loco parentis</u> has been used in some instances to assert school authority when it conflicts with parental authority or students' rights.

Although most commentators agree that <u>in loco parentis</u> is somewhat obsolete as a touchstone for school policy, its vestiges remain. Some schools and teachers, after observing contemporary cautions about due process hold the view that the responsibility of the school in providing discipline carries more weight than student or parental rights. The school's need to be the paramount party in discipline, they would say, is not only historically derived but in accord with educational theory.

A fifth, less developed, point of view about discipline has emerged during the 1970s. Based on the concepts of entitlement, in this case to an appropriate state-supported education, this perspective regards discipline in schools as a legal issue.[10] Disciplinary exclusion, especially the more severe forms, becomes a denial of the right to an education and cannot be imposed without due process protection. Although the clients (students) are recognized to be different because of age and experience, the overall contours of the discipline system should reflect the constitutional rights of students. They are entitled to an education, and efforts to remove them from an educational setting through suspension or expulsion, for example, must be carried out with due regard for those rights.

Within this perspective, there is a great deal of disagreement as to how extensive the protections should be and whether the extension of a formal justice model into schools will result in deadlock and undesirable adversarial relationships, on the one hand, or a greater sense of community and fairness, on the other. There is also concern with whether legal rights for students in schools should focus mainly on suspension and expulsion or be broadly defined to encompass routine student representation in rule-making and enforcement. How pervasive, in other words, should legal rights protections for students be? To what extent should formal legalism imbue school discipline?

There are, of course, still other ways of looking at discipline, and within each of the five identified ways, there are numerous points of view. Nevertheless, these five ways of regarding discipline are the main vantage points expressed in the educational, social science, and legal literature.

Since these five major ways of looking at discipline are considerably at variance--and since there are value judgments involved with each--there is a potentially large community of disagreement about the subject. With so much disagreement about the aims of discipline, it is not surprising that there should be a great deal of controversy about the desired characteristics of the disciplinary system. For example, to an exponent of the moral order perspective, student participation in school decision making is an integral part of the development of the individual's sense of responsibility toward the larger group. Such activity would be meaningful and desirable. To someone seeing discipline as part of the organization's needs, student participation in decision making is desirable as part of social control of students, providing a sense of integration for the governed. Quite the reverse, the critics of schooling in capitalist society would respond. Student participation in decision making is at best illusory, and at worst deceitful, in that it provides the fiction of influence. Student participation in institutional decisions should be avoided because it is cooptation at best. Those who stress the in loco parentis role see school decision making by students as appropriate, within limits. But adults (the school administrators and staff) know best. The school, as an arm of the state, has special parental-type authority over students, and student participation in decision making may be permitted in that context. Finally, for those concerned with the justice-in-schools approach, student participation in decision making, in that it mirrors principles of representation, is desirable.

Proponents of these various viewpoints in many instances are talking past one another. With values so much at variance with one another, their reactions to the empirical world of discipline are widely distributed, and issues such as how much discipline is too much discipline seem insoluble. Disagreement about the role or function of discipline has also tended both to inhibit empirical study of discipline in school settings and to prevent closer correspondence between understanding reality and shaping policy to fit it.

B. Definitions of Discipline

Another major issue has stalked the empirical study of discipline--disagreement about what discipline is. Where do the boundaries of discipline lie? Is discipline the recording of punishments for infractions of school rules? Must the rules be clearly expressed, or may they be implicit? Must the punishment be so identified, or can sarcasm or snubbing be considered discipline? These are the types of questions raised about discipline when it is narrowly defined.

Or is discipline better defined very broadly? Should it include the structuring of the curriculum, for example? If schools offer only preacademic and general courses to the exclusion of vocationally oriented teaching, are they exercising a subtle form of discipline? Perhaps the utilization of standardized testing, with its emphasis on uniformity, should be considered a form of discipline. Some groups perform less well on standardized tests, and therefore the decision of a school to rely on tests can be interpreted as an unwarranted effort to standardize students. Even the decision to require school attendance for those of certain ages might be seen as a form of discipline. Boundaries among activities within schools are very permeable, so that broad definitions of discipline include almost the whole range of school activities. Grading, curriculum, testing, streaming, and special programming can all be considered forms of discipline.[11]

In this book we see discipline as the formal system involving school rules, who breaks them, and what punishments occur. It includes such issues as who makes and enforces rules, who is caught for transgressing rules, who is punished and how, and how the various parties in the school perceive the discipline system. On the continuum of discipline definitions, we lean toward the narrower.

At the same time, we recognize that none of these phenomena exists in isolation. It may be observed which rules are broken, but it may not be so clear why the rules were made or by whom. Similarly, who broke the rules is a different question from who is caught for breaking the rules and also from the question of who is punished for breaking the rules. Discipline events which appear to have discrete beginnings and endings are usually embedded in a more general context.

The events on which we focus do not occur in isolation from the other social relationships of the school. This study presents discipline against a sociological background of administration/staff sharing of power and definition of roles, teacher colleagiality and communication, school/community relations, and student perceptions of their role. We see discipline as a system of relationships and events that grow from and illuminate the functioning of the total school system.

At a general level the things the public tends to care about when considering discipline are how much misbehavior is going on, who is breaking the rules and why, and what is the school doing about rule-breaking. We address these concerns, as well as presenting our sociological approach to discipline.

We believe that discipline should be conceptualized in a framework which balances the need for order in schools with the need for individual student/teacher autonomy. There is by no means much agreement among school personnel on the amount of order needed in schools. Part of the reason that discipline is so infrequently discussed in schools is related to the conflict between order and autonomy.

Discipline as Disorder. While we see discipline as part of the total organizational structure of schools, this view is not common in most studies of the topic. Most of the literature on discipline is confined to questions about exclusionary discipline and school crime. These are, because of the severity of both crime in school and exclusion from school, simply the most visible parts of the iceberg.

So far as exclusionary discipline is concerned, the focus of empirical studies has generally been on the frequency with which children are suspended and whether suspensions have been used in a racially discriminatory manner. The Children's Defense Fund studies revealed very large numbers of children (two million) losing eight million school days a year because of suspensions.[12] A study conducted in Milwaukee reported suspension rates of 21–23 percent over a three-year period, with the rate in senior high schools about 30 percent and the rate in junior high schools about 50 percent.[13] Although most of the studies of suspension have been carried out in metropolitan schools, a few have focused on patterns in other-sized cities and in rural areas. Data from 80 school districts in Ohio indicate that having a high percentage of suspensions is not at all confined to major cities, and that about one in ten students is suspended in an average year.[14] A statewide study in Wisconsin revealed suspension percentages of 24 percent for metropolitan areas, 7 percent for suburbs, 15 percent for sizable cities, and 3 percent for essentially rural areas.[15]

Suspensions, then, in several studies have been demonstrated to be fairly common. The empirical studies do not seem to support consistent interpretations about differential suspension use in urban/rural settings or about suspension use in junior/middle rather than senior high schools.

School crime figures, based on a large nationwide sample of schools, reveal that eight percent of principals believe

that there are serious crime problems in their schools, with
principals in large cities quite a bit more likely to report
serious problems than administrators elsewhere. For the
typical secondary student there is one chance in nine of
having something small in value stolen in a month, one
chance in 80 of being attacked, one chance in 200 of being
robbed. A teacher has one chance in eight of having something small in value stolen in a month, one chance in 200 of
being attacked, one chance in 167 of being robbed. These
are alarming and depressing figures, but the study in which
they are reported concludes that crime figures are stabilized
or improving, rather than worsening.[16] Another study,
based on surveys of principals in Maryland, presents similar
results. Only a small percentage of those interviewed said
discipline matters in their secondary schools were serious, or
that misbehaviors of a threatening or dangerous nature
occurred more than infrequently. Principals from more
urbanized areas reported greater discipline difficulties than
others.[17]

These data about suspensions and school safety, however, need to be seen as part of the total functioning of the
school. We need to be able to sort out the milieu in which
suspension occurs, the alternatives to suspension, the lesser
penalties, the role of the repeater student, the identity of
the enforcers, the nature of the student offenses, and the
perception of the school and the students about the efficacy
of punishment.

C. Methodology and Research Organization

Since we believed that studying a more limited topic,
such as the presence of violence in the school, would present only a partial reflection of discipline, we chose a more
encompassing research conceptualization and methodology.
Our study is based on an interdisciplinary approach, blend-
ing the social sciences with the disciplines of law and education. This interdisciplinary approach stemmed from the
interests of the research team and from an effort to concep-
tualize discipline as more than an isolated series of events.
Because metropolitan schools have received more attention
than others vis-a-vis discipline, we chose to conduct our
study in both urban and rural schools.

In Middle City, a Wisconsin community with a population
of about 100,000 persons, we closely examined discipline in
five public senior and junior high schools using a variety of
complementary techniques. The primary focus of our study
is these urban schools, although we replicated our analysis
in a regional rural school (grades 7-12) to detect

urban/rural differences.   Since the schools in which the study was conducted have very small minority percentages, we are able to study discipline patterns without the complications of serious racial tension.

As our concern was with the sociology of discipline, we elaborated and implemented a complex research design.   The research strategy utilized in-school anthropological observation, lasting several weeks in each school, and occurring at two different times in each, extensive interviewing, and administering complex survey instruments to large numbers of teachers and students.   The anthropological emphasis of our study was developed with the recognition that some of the very best work about schooling has been done by scholars concerned with social dynamics in schools.   We recognized, however, that interviewing and observation alone were not satisfactory to establish discipline patterns.   Thus, we utilized extensive questionnaires for students and teachers.

The major activities at each site included structured interviews with all administrators, surveys of all teachers, stratified random surveys of students in grades 7-12, semi-structured interviews with students, teachers, counselors, and other school personnel, examination of school reports to central school administration authorities, and examination of within-school discipline records.[18]

Over 200 persons were interviewed; interview notes were taken and transcribed.   Approximately 1,500 students and 220 teachers were surveyed.   We read city school board minutes for an extended period to assess the level of community concern about discipline and read local newspaper coverage of education issues for a period of two years.   School newspapers were also examined.   Finally, we spent approximately one month carrying out school-based observation, visiting offices, classrooms, teacher lounges, detention rooms, and public areas inside and around the schools.

The questionnaires which were used with teachers and students were mainly concerned with assessing the correlates of misbehavior and attitudes in the school, with special emphasis on behavior patterns.   Both students and teachers were also asked about their knowledge of state laws and state department of education regulations on discipline. Background information was obtained, as well as career information for teachers.

Among the teachers 80 percent returned the questionnaires, and among the students 92 percent completed usable surveys.   Both groups completed the questionnaires in school, and both groups were told in advance only that their school was participating in a research study being conducted

in association with the state university and approved by
local administrators. The surveys were administered after
the observation and interview phases were completed.

Survey data were collected in 1977-78, and newspa-
per/school board coverage in the period 1976-79. Although
the study in Rural Place was carried out subsequent to the
study phase in the urban schools, the intervening time was
brief, and there was no evidence that anyone in the rural
school system had talked to those in Middle City.
Moreover, Rural Place is in a different part of the state and
contamination seems unlikely to have taken place.

In neither system was there any evidence that school
personnel had significantly modified their behavior in
anticipation of the study or during its conduct, although of
course there may have been slight changes. Our project
staff was sizable, but it could not work in all schools simultaneously. Thus, advance information may have caused some
day-to-day behavior changes. Observations began six weeks
before the survey team visited the schools. This was done
to accustom the school personnel to having researchers in
their midst.

D.   Organization of Our Findings

The major questions on which the study focuses, as indicated above, are all concerned with how the discipline system is integrated with and has developed from the total
organization of the school. Our efforts are designed to work
toward the development of a sociology of discipline, and from
this base to develop policy suggestions for discipline. We
are not simply saying "this is the way discipline is" in public secondary schools. We attempt, rather, to indicate how
the empirical behaviors perceived as discipline derive from
institutional and social-psychological constraints and the
milieu of schooling, and then to discuss how schools can
achieve a better fit between what they generally intend and
what they actually do. Chapter 2 defines further the key
concepts which are central to this work--order, autonomy
and discipline. We suggest that schools which focus exces-
sively on order may, paradoxically, achieve greater disorder
than other schools with less rigorous regimes. While schools
seldom make a conscious choice, personnel and school boards
have the opportunity to select the degree of order or autonomy which they wish to promote. This choice is related to
how "effective" the schools will be in teaching students.

Chapter 3 is an overview of discipline problems. It is
mainly concerned with three questions: (1) How much misbehavior is there in schools and how serious is it? (2) What

is the locus of control in the discipline system? (3) What penalties are used and under what circumstances? For the most part, we report a strong consensus about how the discipline systems works and a community of shared expectations about the parameters of the system.

Students, teachers, and administrators may have the same understanding of a system, just as most Americans share an understanding of the United States Internal Revenue Code. But they may differ in their assessments of how fair it is, just as citizens vary in their opinions about taxing systems. And there may be unfairness in the system, whether it is recognized by parties directly affected or not. It is questions of fairness that Chapter 4 addresses. At an obvious level it asks whether people think the system of discipline is fair. Does it discriminate against certain groups, and if discipline is not dispensed in an evenhanded manner, how much do school people mind? Are they correct in their assessments of who benefits from the system? And, at a more theoretical level, under what circumstances do students receive different treatment, and to what ends do different treatments lead? The issues of fairness, of course, underlie U.S. Supreme Court decisions about discipline and much state-level policy making.

Chapter 5 turns to the more anguished side of discipline problems--the troubled student, the troubled school, the troubled teacher. It examines the amount of confirmation for "bad boy" stereotypes to be found when detailed socioeconomic data about students are available, and suggests the links between school-based expectations of students and their behavior. Turning to schools, which vary in their self-assessments as instructional environments, the chapter shows how much correspondence exists between the assessment by teachers that a school is not a good place to teach, and day-in, day-out misbehavior. The ability of schools to foster myths and the utility of myths is also discussed. The final section of Chapter 5 discussed why some teachers have so much more trouble with discipline than others, using a large array of socioeconomic and school role variables to explain the differential experiences of teachers.

Building on the findings of Chapter 3 and 5, Chapter 6 is a close study of the role of formal disciplinary procedure in schools. Focusing mainly on suspensions, the chapter outlines the purposes believed served by suspensions, the nature of events leading to suspension, the actual process of suspension, and the effects of suspensions. All of these issues are raised in the context of the impact of Goss v. Lopez (1975) in which the Supreme Court required that public schools provide students facing suspension with a statement of charges and a chance to tell their sides of the

story. How much of the Court's intent is realized in the
schools, we ask, and what does this suggest about the role
of legalism in public schooling?

The final chapter ties empirical findings about misbehavior, penalties, fairness, troubled actors, and formal justice as discussed in Chapters 3 through 6 to the perspectives in this and the next chapter. Looking at discipline as
we have defined it, and with emphasis on the importance of
conceptualizing discipline as a creative tension between
autonomy and order, we find systematic evidence of both
success and failure in the way the discipline system operates
in schools. Looking at the problems or failures in the narrow sense is not, we suggest, helpful. Discipline failures
are system failures--that is, discipline problems represent
hard structural problems or serious educational issues in
schools. They should not be conceptualized just as discipline issues. Chapter 7 suggests, on the basis of our view
of discipline, how schools might best go about addressing
some of the problems, expressed partially as disciplinary
incidents, that plague them. It also considers the kinds of
obstacles that lie between problem analysis and problem
address or solution.

Our aims in writing this book have been twofold: first,
to describe the discipline activities in a school to show how
particular events arise from the general patterns of schools,
relations, and second, given the correspondence between
particular events and general patterns, to suggest perspectives for changing "misbehaviors." With some careful thinking about their goals and their resources, schools can, we
suggest, both understand better why students misbehave
and begin to affect their disciplinary climates.

NOTES

[1]These have been the results of Gallup polls about education, 1974 to the present. The National Education Association's 1979 Nationwide Teacher Opinion Poll found almost
unanimous agreement about the need for stricter discipline in
schools and for research about discipline.

[2]Although a small literature about burnout in human
services organizations has developed in the last few years,
no empirical study has been conducted of the factors leading
to burnout (as distinguished from turnover) in schools. The
teacher educational journals contain frequent profiles of
teachers moving to other careers after a decade in education, and the reasons most often cited relate to problems

with student discipline and disinterest. See "The Pain of Teacher Burnout: A Case History," Phi Delta Kappan 61 (December, 1979); Christine Maslach, "Burnout: A Social-Psychological Analysis," paper presented to the American Psychological Association, August, 1977.

[3]For the most part such articles focus on metropolitan settings and emphasize physical safety problems children experience both in school and on the way to and from school.

[4]Alfred S. Alschuler, School Discipline: A Socially Literate Solution (New York: McGraw-Hill, 1980); Walter Doyle, "Helping Teachers Manage Classrooms," NASSP Bulletin 59 (December, 1975); Ronald L. Abrell, "Classroom Discipline Without Punishment," Clearinghouse 50 (December, 1976); Marvin L. Grantham and Clifton S. Harris, Jr., "A Faculty Trains Itself to Improve Student Discipline," Phi Delta Kappan 57 (June, 1976); Emery Stoops and Joyce King-Stoops, Discipline or Disaster? (Bloomington, Indiana: Phi Delta Kappa Educational Foundation, 1975); J.S. Kounin, Discipline and Group Management in Classrooms (New York: Holt, Rinehart, Winston, 1970). See also P. Susan Mamchak and Steven R. Mamchak, The New Psychology of Classroom Discipline and Control (West Nyack, N.Y.: Parker Publishing Co., 1981); Charles H. Wolfgang and Carl D. Glickman, Solving Discipline Problems: Strategies for Classroom Teachers (Boston: Allyn and Bacon, 1982); Daniel L. Duke (ed.) Helping Teachers Manage Classrooms (Alexandria, Va.: Association for Supervision and Curriculum Development, 1982); Eugene R. Howard, "School Discipline--Helping the Teacher: Improving Discipline by Improving the School," National Association of Secondary School Principals, Reston, Va., 1982; Kevin J. Sevick, "Disruptive Student Behavior in the Classroom: What Research Says to the Teacher," National Education Association, Washington, D.C., 1980; William W. Wayson et al, "Handbook for Developing Schools with Good Discipline," Phi Delta Kappa, Bloomington, Indiana, 1982.

[5]The most notable publication for presenting materials on alternative discipline methods was prepared by the Southeastern Public Education Program of the American Friends Service Committee in Columbia, South Carolina. The publication, Creative Discipline, was published in 1977-1979. Its best articles were published in book form, School Discipline, by the parent organization, 1981.

[6]See the work of Lawrence Kohlberg, "Stage and Sequence: The Cognitive-Developmental Approach to Socialization," in Handbook of Socialization Theory and

Research, D. Goslin (ed.) (Chicago: Rand–McNally, 1969);
Lawrence Kohlberg, "From Is to Ought...," in Cognitive De-
velopment and Epistemology, T. Mischel (ed.) (New York:
Academic Press, 1971); Lawrence Kohlberg and Rochelle
Mayer, "Development as the Aim of Education," Harvard
Educational Review 42 (November, 1972); Ronald Galbraith
and Thomas Jones, Moral Reasoning: A Teaching Handbook
for Adapting Kohlberg to the Classroom (Anoka, Minnesota:
Greenhaven Press, 1976); John Martin Rich, Discipline and
Authority in School and Family (Lexington: Lexington Books,
1982).

[7]See J.S. Packard, "Schools as Work Organizations,"
Paper read to the Symposium on Organizational Characteris-
tics of Schools, University of California at Santa Barbara,
Feb. 10, 1977; L.D. Spence, Y. Takei and F.M. Sim, "Con-
ceptualizing Loose Coupling: Believing is Seeing or the
Garbage Can as Myth and Ceremony," Paper read to Ameri-
can Sociological Association, 1978; Melvin Tumin, "Schools as
Social Organizations," in Perspectives on Organizations: The
School as a Social Organization, R.G. Corwin, R. A.
Edelfelt, T.E. Andrews, and B.L. Bryant (eds.)
(Washington: American Association of Colleges for Teacher
Education, and Association of Teacher Educators, 1977); Dan
C. Lortie, "Two Anomalies and Three Perspectives: Some
Observations on School Organization," in Perspectives on
Organizations: The School as a Social Organization, R.G.
Corwin, R.A. Edelfelt, T.E. Andrews, and B.L. Bryan
(eds.) (Washington: American Association of Colleges for
Teacher Education and Association of Teacher Educators,
1977); Matthew B. Miles, "Mapping the Common Properties of
Schools," Improving Schools: Using What We Know, Rolf
Lehming and Michael Kane (eds.) (Beverly Hills: Sage Pub-
lications, 1981).

[8]See Samuel Bowles and Herbert Gintis, Schooling in
Capitalist America: Educational Reform and the Contra-
dictions of Economic Life (New York: Basic Books, 1976);
Michael R. Olneck and David B. Bills, "What Makes Sammy
Run? An Empirical Assessment of the Bowles-Gintis Corre-
spondence Theory," American Journal of Education (Nov.,
1980); James Rosenbaum, Making Inequality: The Hidden
Curriculum of High School Tracking (New York: John Wiley
and Sons, 1976); Paul Willis, Learning to Labour: How
Working Class Kids Get Working Class Jobs (Westmead,
England: Saxon House, 1977); Marvin Lazerson, "Revisionism
and American Educational History," Harvard Educational
Review 43 (1973).

[9]Edward C. Bolmeier, Legality of Student Disciplinary Practices (Charlottesville, Va.: The Michie Co., 1976), Chapter 2.

[10]For an early critique of this view see David L. Kirp, "Proceduralism and Bureaucracy: Due Process in the School Setting," Stanford Law Review 28 (1976).

[11]Much of the literature that takes this view is part of the revisionist school, which considers the whole of the school as an institution with a distinctive cultural role. Specific aspects of the schooling process are not differentiated; rather, the whole of the experience of schooling is treated together.

[12]Children's Defense Fund, Children Out of School in America (Washington, D.C.: Washington Research Project, Inc., 1974); Children's Defense Fund, School Suspensions: Are They Helping Children? (Washington: Washington Research Project, Inc., 1975).

[13]Community Relations-Social Development Commission, "Special Student Concerns Project: Phase I Research Report," (Milwaukee County, Wisconsin, 1978).

[14]Children Out of School in Ohio (Columbus: Citizens' Council for Ohio Schools, 1977).

[15]Ellen Jane Hollingsworth, "Fairness and Discretion: Exemptions in Wisconsin," Report to the National Institute of Education, January, 1981.

[16]National Institute of Education, Violent Schools--Safe Schools (Washington, D.C., 1977). Also see "Violence in the Schools: How Much? What to Do?" Research Action Brief, Number 17 (ERIC, 1981).

[17]Maryland Association of Secondary School Principals, "Final Report of the Task Force on Educational Programs for Disruptive Youth," Maryland Department of Education, 1976. Also see Thomas A. DiPrete, "Discipline and Order in American High School," Report of National Opinion Research Center, November, 1981.

[18]Over 100 people were interviewed, with interviews lasting between 15 and 45 minutes. Those interviewed included social workers, librarians, cooks, janitors, student body leaders, students identified as troublemakers,

counselors, and students encountered at random in congregate settings.

Chapter 2

ORDER, AUTONOMY, DISCIPLINE AND LEARNING

The research design and the principal research findings of this study concern the connections among order, autonomy, discipline, and learning. Because these concepts are often used with overlapping meanings, our discussion of them must be more precise (and artificial) than ordinary speech.

Order can be defined as the condition of being "on educational task." Order in schools is <u>educationally organized behavior</u>. The so-called effective schools literature shows that the effective school must be an orderly school at two levels.[1] At the individual level, students must be doing educational work rather than being absent from school (physically or mentally) or wasting their time on noneducational activities, such as waiting in line or cleaning their desks. At the collective or environmental level, the school must be a comfortable place to think and work, free from violence, harassment, and noisy distractions. Of course, order does not produce learning by itself. The assigned educational tasks must be meaningful and productive. Thus, order is a necessary but not a sufficient condition for effectiveness.

The opposite of order may be either lethargy or disruption. Lethargy is passive disorder, such activities as tuning out and refusal to do homework. Disruption is active disorder, including fighting, skipping, cutting, smoking, wandering, loitering, and making noise.

In principle, the exact line between passive and active disorder is totally unclear. Theoretically, skipping class could be seen as active (doing something else) or passive (refusing to participate), as more like talking (active) or daydreaming (passive). School discipline resolves this theoretical uncertainty by defining certain conduct as active disruption. In effect, school discipline is the system for defining and sanctioning active disruptions of the educational order.

Two more concepts remain to be defined. Learning is self explanatory. Autonomy is freedom, the right of individuals (students, teachers) to do what they choose, be where they choose, wear what they choose, and so on.

Two basic relationships among these central concepts which we just defined were discovered by our research: the effect of learning on order and the effect of discipline on order.

A. Order, Learning and Discipline

The Effect of Learning on Order. Our data suggest (but do not prove) a causal relationship running from the learning experience to the existence of order and disruptions. When the learning experience is satisfactory, order results; unsatisfactory learning brings disruptions. Disruptions, of course, bring discipline. This relationship may be surprising. In effect, schools which are bad end up punishing their students. As used here, "bad" means simply a negative learning experience, without implying anything about who might be responsible for the experience or what could be done about it.

One suggestion of this phenomenon which we will be reporting in our data is the pervasive influence of class and occupation. Students bound for the working class have less to gain from academic training. They seem more prone to disruptions, and they seem to make it harder for college-oriented teachers to have high expectations of them. Low expectations are frustrating and perhaps offensive, leading to a bad relationship between school and student, and therefore to disruptions. The effective schools literature shows that it is possible to have high expectations and an orderly school for working-class students. Our research shows (in a less direct way) that is possible for low expectations to bring disorder and, presumably, a less effective education.

Another indication of the link between poor learning and disorder is the role of individual troubled students (see Chapter 5). Troubled students are not just disruptive; they are alienated from education and the school as an organization. They do not participate in academics or extracurricular activities and have low opinions of both their school and the usefulness of education in general. Again we see the basic relationship--those who are not learning, who are not engaged in the educational enterprise, are more likely to disrupt the educational order and be disciplined for it.

The Effect of Discipline on Order. The primary emphasis in our research was on school discipline as a differentiated subsystem or activity of the educational enterprise, a subsystem with a myriad of relationships to the educational enterprise as a whole. For this reason, the evidence we found for an effect of discipline on order is much more direct than the evidence for an effect of learning on order.

In general, we found that "excessive discipline" leads to educational disorder. There are two levels of this finding. The first level is discipline as disorder. Disciplinary punishments like suspension and expulsion take students off educational task. If there is really no important reason for punishing the students in this way, as when the offenses are trivial, discipline is simply "shooting itself in the foot." The second level involves a form of backlash. Unfair, excessive, and arbitrary school discipline seems to generate various kinds of resistance, e.g., frustration, resentment, game playing. Just as a poor learning experience can lead to disruptions, so can a poor disciplinary experience.

Some schools seem to punish students for activities that do not threaten the educational enterprise. Since the punishments often consist of removing the student from school (suspension or expulsion), the discipline is both unnecessary and self defeating. Most disciplinary sanctions are imposed for what seem to be relatively harmless acts: smoking, talking, wearing the wrong clothes, and the like. Such behavior cannot be classified as educationally trivial (see Chapter 3). Indeed, all of these behaviors represent disruptions of the educational order. The problem is the nature and severity of the punishments imposed for such conduct and the absence of nondisciplinary methods of social control. Kicking students out of school for irritating misbehavior seems self defeating. There ought to be a better way, and the schools which have the heaviest hand seem to give the least thought to alternatives. Disciplining these relatively harmless acts is not wrong; but the punishment can be excessive.

Another example of excessive discipline is unfair discipline (see Chapter 4). When students are singled out for punishment because of some status, they are deprived of education without any corresponding gain in educational order. When students are protected from punishment because of some privileged status, such as athletic team participation, educational order is the loser.

Our findings on excessive discipline of minor offenses cannot be considered strictly scientific. They involve an element of judgment. Defenders of harsh discipline claim a need for special and general deterrence (punishing the particular offender and letting others know that they will be punished for similar conduct). The findings reported below about the second level (backlash) suggest exactly the opposite. Excessive discipline produces more, rather than less, misbehavior.

The second level of the effect of discipline on order is the causative influence of unfair and excessive discipline on the occurrence of disorders. Once again, our evidence is not conclusive. A fair interpretation of the data, however, is that unfair and "repressive" disciplinary regimes generate frustration and unhappiness on the part of students which, like the frustration from poor learning, expresses itself in disruptive behavior. The primary evidence is the existence of the "troubled school" (see Chapter 5), although the troubled school also becomes a kind of paradigm for interpreting much of the data in other chapters.

The troubled school shows us that the disciplinary mentality can get badly out of hand. If the effective schools literature convinces us that the school "as an organization" can have an ethos or culture supportive of learning, our findings on the troubled school suggest the possibility of a self-destructive disciplinary culture. The troubled school is characterized by distrust and overreaction. School authorities overestimate the amount of disorder and regard students as dangerous. The students feel mistrusted and rebellious and in fact do misbehave somewhat more than students in nontroubled schools. Troubled schools have a siege mentality based on a myth of massive disruption. Some disruption is present, but the reaction is excessive.

Summary: Order, Autonomy and Learning. The idea of excessive discipline raises the question, excessive compared to what? The answer seems to be excessive as compared with what is necessary for effective education. Discipline seems to "work" as long as it has a good reason. This relationship has two fascinating implications. On the one hand, it ties the idea of effective discipline back to the idea of effective schools and creates a startling symmetry with the first influence discussed in this section. Earlier we said that an ineffective school creates discipline problems. Here we are saying that discipline beyond the needs of effective schooling creates its own problems. Again, we can say this partly as a matter of definition or judgment, because we are willing to characterize certain sanctions as unnecessary and educationally harmful. It is as though the ideal of effective schooling acts as an equilibrium device on the system of school discipline, as though people know instinctively what they are in school for.

Excessive discipline also presents a fascinating connection with constitutional law, specifically the fourteenth amendment rights to substantive and procedural due process. Substantive due process evaluates any government policy according to whether it is serving some legitimate governmental purpose.[2] With regard to minimum competency achievement testing, for example, substantive due process requires that students not be flunked for nonperformance unless they have an educational alternative (e.g., remedial instruction).[3] Arguably, there is no good government purpose for testing if flunking students leads to no better, or perhaps even worse, education.[4] Procedural due process, the other important provision of the fourteenth amendment, is also based on the requirement of a good reason. When both sides of a story are heard, it is more likely that a decision will be based on real and significant facts.[5]

In a surprising way, then, our research demonstrates a connection between the effective schools literature and the rather analytical precepts of constitutional law. At a very general level, both procedural and substantive due process require that liberty and property should not be taken by the state without a good reason. Understandably, courts have not been willing to intrude very far into the educational process by defining what constitutes a "good reason." Our research suggests that the effective school is the good reason and that, to the extent the courts do not intrude, the requirement of a good reason is self enforcing. The conclusion might be thought of in this way: since the effective school involves a considerable degree of order, it also must take away some of the autonomy of its participant teachers and students. Indeed, lacking a minimum of educational order, the autonomy of some students to engage in disruptions impairs the autonomy of other students to engage in learning (itself a form of autonomy). However, when more autonomy is taken than is required for effective education, all sorts of problems result. The excessive punishments needlessly deprive the punished students of education and actually provoke disruptions in the form of resistance, thereby depriving other students of autonomy.

The key to all of this is the idea of taking away some autonomy on behalf of order, but not too much. Perhaps the greatest challenge to consensus about excessive discipline is the existence of competing educational philosophies, some more strict and others more permissive. Schools that are all apparently effective differ in the amount of order they consider important, and therefore in the amount of autonomy which they consider appropriate to take (and allow). How, then, is it possible to specify how much order is enough order, how much autonomy is too little autonomy?

B.   Order-Autonomy Trade-Offs

We think that the idea of "excessive" discipline is per-
fectly compatible with effective schools emphasizing different
amounts of order.   All that is required is specifying a <u>zone</u>
of educationally effective order, within which various blends
of order and autonomy are possible, versus another zone of
excessive or insufficient discipline which actually reduces
educationally effective order.   In other words, a lot of discipline is not necessarily the same as a lot of order, and a
lack of discipline does not automatically produce more student autonomy.   The characteristics of the discipline system
need to be differentiated from the effects which they are
proposed to produce.

To show the conceptual possibility of this distinction
(though not here its substantive content), let us try to be
somewhat more formal about the relationship between order
and autonomy, expressing that relationship in graphic terms.
Conceptually, the relationship between order and autonomy is
expressed in Figure 1.   The order variable measures the degree of educationally effective order.   The autonomy variable
measures the freedom of students (and teachers) from regulation (autonomy is, therefore, freedom from rules and sanctions).   A high-order school would be one in which order is
highly prized and clearly evident; a high-autonomy school
would be one in which relatively few aspects of behavior
were regulated.

FIGURE 1

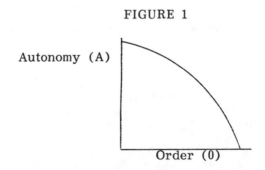

These two variables are related in that (1) there is a
negative trade-off between them (in order to get more of
one, you must have less of the other), and (2) extreme
amounts of autonomy or order are very expensive in terms of
the other variable.   To get, for example, the highest possible amount of autonomy, perhaps absolute freedom from any
rule or sanction, it is necessary to give up a great deal of
order.   The converse is also true.

Perhaps the meaning can be clarified by putting three typical kinds of schools on the curve, as in Figure 2.

FIGURE 2

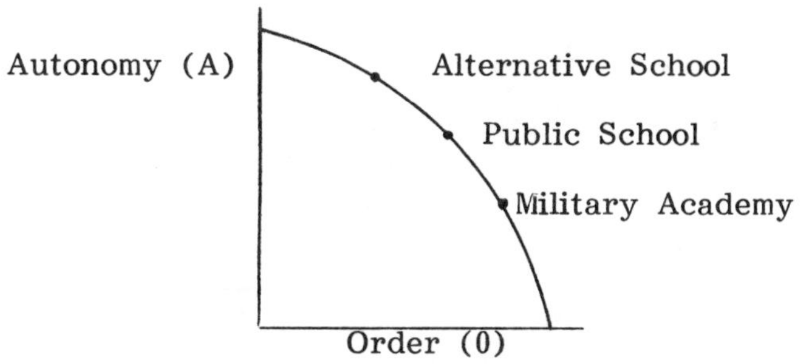

The three kinds of schools differ in the balance of order and autonomy they seek and often achieve. In alternative schools, freedom from rules is greatly valued, and a certain amount of order is not perceived to be necessary to a good education. In the military academy, freedom from rules is not considered very valuable; in fact, a certain amount of rote obedience improves a young person's character and intellectual power. Moreover, even small amounts of distraction from organized tasks (disorder) are likely to be seen as quite harmful to the achievement of those tasks.

Nothing about the figures says whether one approach or the other is valid. One may be quite wrong (e.g., military academies may produce adults who are incapable of self-imposed orderliness); both may be right in different ways (e.g., the students have special strengths in different kinds of real-life situations); or both could be wrong. The graph merely says that discipline policies tend to be consciously chosen according to a perceived autonomy/order trade-off.

How a particular school, rule, practice, or punishment fits the idealized trade-off between autonomy and order is an entirely different matter. In practice, an actual school may be below not on the curve, a position from which it is theoretically easy to change. Graphically, the following is portrayed in Figure 3--a school, X, is well below its possible frontier of autonomy and order with the consequence that the school can increase both autonomy and order at the same time (the middle arrow), increase order at no cost to autonomy, or vice versa (the side arrows). A move toward a situation in which one good can be increased without any cost to the other is called a "pareto optimal" move, and the situation which is achieved, reaching any place along the curve, is called "pareto optimality." All three arrows thus represent "pareto optimal" moves.

FIGURE 3

Three Possible "Moves"

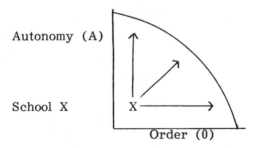

Autonomy (A)

School X

Order (O)

Concrete examples of the moves will doubtless be help-ful. Let us say that there is a school with the following characteristics. A great deal of disorder (X) exists (dis-ruption of all kinds), so that the school is low on the order scale. There is a repressive disciplinary authority which doles out a multitude of serious punishments, with indiffer-ence as to whether they fall on real perpetrators, except that strong patterns of racial discrimination exist. This "reign of terror" has permitted little student autonomy and probably would fan the flames of disorder by creating stu-dent resentment. Assuming that this school can devise a means of doing so, the following "moves" or institutional changes are open to it:

(1) A vertical move (more autonomy, same amount of order). Let us say that the authorities simply eliminated some of the more repressive disciplinary policies, without al-tering the disruptions in the school. We would then see a rather disorderly school in which the students did not suffer autonomy losses from the authorities. Keep in mind that, because of the disorder, this school also might not be a place in which one learns very much.

(2) A horizontal move (more order, no more aut-onomy). Suppose school authorities could reduce the dis-order by an equally strict but more effective discipline system, a kind of reform school approach. This could result in an orderly school but one in which the students had a low degree of autonomy from authority (e.g., almost all aspects of what a student did would be regulated, and infractions of even minor rules would be severely punished). Again, such a school should be imagined as giving even less autonomy than a military academy, being about equally orderly, and not necessarily being a very good place for learning.

(3) A diagonal, or "northeast" move. It might be pos-sible to increase order and autonomy simultaneously by

enacting a discipline policy which was firm but intelligently directed toward important matters and administered fairly. Autonomy would increase because the improved discipline policy would be a greater deterrent without causing resentment.

In a sense, the frontier (curve) on the graphs represent the maximum degree to which discipline policies can be "thought through." A school's place along the curve depends upon what philosophy is brought to this process of rationalizing discipline, in other words, the relative weights given to order versus autonomy. Therefore, although legitimate disputes exist about which place along the curve produces the best and most learning, everyone on the curve can agree about the ineffectiveness of schools below the curve. Throughout this book we will be concerned, with the kinds of autonomy and order choices the schools have made and the benefits and costs of these choices. In making value judgments, we tend to rely on the kind of "consensus zone" of educationally ineffective discipline just described.

C. A Concluding Note on What the Schools Can't Do

An extremely unfortunate tendency exists today of scapegoating the schools for social problems, especially public schools. The National Commission on Excellence in Education, for example, blamed the schools for declining test scores,[6] without even giving serious consideration to other plausible sources of this phenomenon, such as a culture which glorifies materialistic consumption and individual autonomy rather than intellectual achievement and social cooperation, families made less educationally effective by the need of both parents to work, replacement of reading with T.V. watching, the unavailability of jobs requiring high achievement for most high school graduates, and the allocation of high salaries to jobs producing market goods rather than education.

Our research also has a flavor of criticizing the schools in the sense that we argue for a more educationally effective discipline policy. But we have no basis for saying that all or even most discipline problems are caused by the schools. Indeed, we doubt that this is so. Society brings the raw material of discipline problems into the school in the form of students troubled by their culture, families, local communities, and chances in social and economic life. Schools already do a lot to counteract these problems, and our research does not concern how to do more. Rather, we are concerned with those improvements which can be made by improving discipline policy itself, however small those improvements may be relative to the "total problem." In this, we follow in the tradition of the effective schools literature which broke with the preexisting research tradition on the effect of schooling compared to family background. The effective schools research asked the constructive question, what can schooling do given family background.

Our research does suggest, however, that at least in the schools we studied (schools not faced with the devasting problems of urban poverty) a substantial proportion of discipline problems are "self imposed." Hence, the chances of substantial improvement are reasonably good. The main obstacle to improvement is the difficulty of self improvement. How can schools locked in a subpar disciplinary situation release themselves from their negative dynamics? That discussion is reserved for Chapter 7.

NOTES

[1]In general, see Stewart C. Purkey and Marshall S. Smith, "Effective Schools: A Review." Elementary School Journal 427 (March 1983); Michael Rutter, "School Effects on Pupil Progress: Research Findings and Policy Implications" in Handbook of Teaching and Policy 3, Lee S. Shulman and Gary Sykes, eds., (New York: Longman Press, 1983); Stewart C. Purkey and Marshall S. Smith, "Ends Not Means: The Policy Implications of Effective Schools Research," Working Paper), (Madison: Wisconsin Center For Education Research, August, 1982).

For primary sources, see Wilbur Brookover, et al., School Social Systems and Student Achievement (New York: Praeger, 1979); Michael Rutter et al., Fifteen Thousand Hours (Cambridge: Harvard University Press 1979); Ronald R. Edmonds, "A Report on the Research Project, 'Search for Effective Schools...' and Certain of the Designs for School Improvement That are Associated With the Project," (unpublished report to the National Institute of Education, September, 1981).

[2]"It [substantive due process] bars governmental action deemed arbitrary." Bernard Schwartz, Constitutional Law, A Textbook (New York: MacMillan, 2d ed., 1979). One form of arbitrariness is excessive punishment. See Mark Yudof, "Liability for Constitutional Torts and the Risk Averse Public School Official, So. Cal. Law Rev. 49, (Sept. 1976).

During the "hands off" approach of the post-Lochner era, it has been difficult to identify what the Court might mean by "arbitrary." Since all legislation has some real political purpose, the idea of a law without any purpose is silly. Yet the idea of a "reasonable" or "rational" purpose implies some judicial evaluation of legislative ends, an exercise supposedly abandoned by the Court with its retreat from economic due process. See W. Lockhart, Yale Kamisar, J. Choper, "Four Decades of Judicial Abstention," The American Constitution, Cases and Materials,(St. Paul: West, 1981), pp. 270-72; and Laurence Tribe, "Judicial Abdication After the Collapse of Lochner," American Constitutional Law (Mineola, N.Y.: Foundation Press, 1978), pp. 450-455.

Because of the fear of opening up free-wheeling evaluation of legislative ends, modern substantive due process has tended to be expressed in terms of some preferred right, such as the right to privacy (e.g., abortion), making it indistinguishable from the so-called substantive equal protection. See Moore v. City of East Cleveland, 97 S.Ct. 1932 (1977) ("single family dwelling" in zoning law must include grandparents). The other tendency is to emphasize procedural regularity. See Thompson v. City of Louisville, 362 U.S. 199 (1960) ("shuffling Sam" case: "no evidence" for disturbing the peace).

[3] See Paul Tractenberg, "Testing for Minimum Competency: A Legal Analysis," in Minimum Competency Achievement Testing, Richard M. Jaeger and Carol Tittle eds., (Berkeley: McCutcheon Publishing, 1980).

[4] The substantive content of the idea of "arbitrariness," mentioned in footnote 2 supra, becomes evident here. There are actually several plausible political purposes for flunking students without providing remedial instruction: stigmatizing low achievers, saving money, and satisfying society's concerns about educational quality through ritual compliance. Therefore, if flunking without remediation is deemed arbitrary, it is probably because education is considered some kind of preferred right.

[5] On the instrumental versus dignitary purposes of procedural due process, see Laurence Tribe, American Constitutional Law, fn. 2 supra; Jerry L. Mashaw, "Administrative Due Process: The Quest for a Dignitary Theory," Boston Univ. Law Rev. 61 (July 1981). The Mashaw article points out that procedural due process, like substantive due process, is haunted by the necessity of identifying some substantive reason for the judicial requirement.

[6] National Commission on Excellence in Education, Education Daily 14 (No. 165, August 27, 1981). One of the concerns of the Commission was higher standards. For a

comment on the report of the staff of the Commission, see
"Academic Courses Lose Favor," New York Times, April 26,
1983, at 17.

[7]See the first chapters in both the Brookover and
Rutter books, fn 1 supra, and the Rutter essay in the
Shulman and Sykes collection, fn. 1 supra, at p. 5-8.

Chapter 3

SCHOOL MISBEHAVIOR AND PUNISHMENT

Question: Is discipline a problem in your school?
Student 1:   No.
Student 2:   It used to be.   It's better now.   The
             vice-principal has helped.   Essentially,
             I like what he is doing.   I missed 43
             days of school as a sophomore.   Now
             I'm just turned off.   I just want to
             get through with things.
Student 3:   A little bit.   No. Definitely yes on
             the junior high level.
Student 4:   Yes.   Because of the vice-principal.
             The open campus is just making things
             worse!

Are things really out of hand in schools so far as discipline is concerned?   Are teachers facing problems involving violence and threats to their safety on a daily basis?   There is much confusion about these issues, as the student responses above indicate.   To answer these questions, we turn to the frequency of misbehavior in schools, how often misbehavior is apprehended, and what the schools do in response.   In other terms we ask to what extent order keeping seems to be a problem and to what extent school responses to misbehavior involve serious autonomy loss for students and teachers.

We first analyze the extent to which the most frequent misbehaviors involve challenges to order maintenance, as opposed to serious crimes. or threats.   Schools, in their concern for maintaining social control, may be rather like the police.   Although the public believes that police spend most of their time enforcing the law (making arrests, conducting investigations), in fact police spend much more time simply maintaining order and responding to trouble spots (e.g., traffic jams, altercations in bars, domestic disturbances). Schools may be much the same. If most of the activities defined as misbehavior or discipline involve fairly humdrum, routine events, school responses presumably will vary accordingly and not involve heavy penalties.

Second, we discuss the range of school responses to misbehavior. A range of nondisciplinary responses or a range of disciplinary actions may greet the same offense. School personnel can substitute nondisciplinary for disciplinary sanctions in order to meet the needs of the school organization. Under some circumstances for example, rigid adherence to a punishment repertory may be awkward for personnel. Such variety in outcomes when misbehavior occurs is a natural outgrowth of the way schools see their order-maintenance function. They have to keep order, but they have other goals which require a large measure of informality and discretion. However, such variation in responses to misbehavior, stemming from the presence of a great deal of uncontrolled discretion, can raise problems of fairness.

A. Frequency of Discipline Problems Reported by Teachers and Students

Much has been written about discipline problems in school, but it is rare that data have been available about the issue. We know little, for example, about the frequency of more serious problems. We also do not know if all teachers see the problems the same way, or if they agree on what to do about them. We do not even know if a few students are causing all the problems. To start to address these concerns, we asked students and teachers in several junior and senior high schools in Middle City to tell us how often they saw certain types of activities occurring (see Table 3-1).

Serious crime and crime threat are present in these schools, as indicated by the frequency indicated for carrying weapons, assaults on teachers, and committing of crimes, although they are not present as everyday occurrences. Much more common are medium-level discipline events--fighting, vandalizing, use of liquor/drugs, and stealing. These are all difficult matters for schools, and a good bit of school energy goes into coping with each one. They can range from being considered obnoxious things to be dealt with, to being considered very disturbing and frightening. But for the most part these are problems which can be settled within

Table 3-1

Frequency of Problems

How often have you seen students doing these things in your school:*

	Students	Teachers
Talking during class	98.8	97.8
Fighting with other students	45.4 (7.0)	44.7 (9.5)
Swearing at a teacher	35.2 (8.0)	43.7 (9.4)
Cheating	79.2	75.4
Setting false alarms	3.7	25.7
Making out	55.2	55.0
Stealing	33.0 (6.0)	36.4 (7.3)
Wandering in halls	88.1	93.0
Gambling	24.5 (6.0)	21.9 (.5)
Assaulting a teacher	12.8 (3.0)	33.4 (0)
Using liquor/drugs	46.5 (21.0)	45.0 (12.6)
Skipping school (truancy)	76.2 (39.0)	86.4 (38.0)
Vandalizing school property	41.4 (13.0)	61.7 (21.3)
Talking back to teacher	80.3	77.7
Possessing weapons	19.2 (6.0)	8.8 (1.1)
Carrying firecrackers	23.8	11.6
Committing a crime	22.1 (6.0)	14.8 (1.7)
Swearing at other students	91.1	81.7
Kissing	70.0	40.7
Throwing things	77.1	74.8
Being unprepared for class	91.3	95.1
N =	1316	184

*Percent responding "frequently" or "sometimes" rather than "rarely" or "not at all" shown. For selected offenses, the percentages answering "frequently" are shown separately in parentheses.

the school, without calling in the police. In these schools the medium-level problems are said to occur "sometimes" and thus do not seem to be much of a threat. Very common misbehaviors, as reported by both teachers and students are talking during class, cheating, wandering in the halls, skipping (truancy), talking back to teachers, students swearing at other students, students being unprepared for class, and

throwing things.[1] These are misbehaviors and may trigger
disciplinary action. But they do not represent real disturbances of the school's social order or educational mission.
In the list of commonplace misbehaviors, skipping school is
the most worrisome to schools.

Comparing student and teacher observations about the
frequency of misbehavior helps highlight the few differences
between the groups.[2] Teachers might be inclined to report
a very disorderly school scene, because of implicit comparison to earlier years in their careers. Or students, especially younger ones, might be inclined to report a world of
chaos, in contrast with elementary school days. For the
most part, this does not occur. As Table 3-1 indicates,
teachers and students are in agreement on which activities
are "everyday" events. Almost everyone thinks there is un-
solicited talking in class, frequently or sometimes; over
three-quarters of each group think there is cheating somewhat frequently. Throwing things and skipping school are
also reported by nearly equal percentages of both groups.

But there are a few real points of difference. Teachers
are quite a bit more likely than students to report assaults,
setting off fire alarms, and vandalism of school property.
Perhaps these differences are because teachers care more
about attacks and vandalism, have better information about
such events, and even try to keep students uninformed
about them. It is not, however, easy to disguise a false
fire alarm, and the considerable difference in student and
teacher reports may indicate mainly that teachers regard fire
alarm setting as a much more serious offense than students
do. It is logical that the more serious an offense is regarded to be, the fewer times it would have to occur in
order to be placed in any given frequency category. Thus,
three murders in one year, in a small town, might logically
be considered "frequent." On the other hand, students are
quite a bit more likely than teachers to report weapons,
firecrackers, crime, and kissing. These are all things students have better reasons to know about, although there
may be some exaggeration stemming from the mystique of
these activities.

Assuming that the more people say that something is
occurring the more frequent it is, these data tell us that
students and teachers commonly experience events such as
being unprepared, wandering in the halls and students
swearing at other students. These are not very serious
offenses; in fact, being unprepared might be classified as an
academic deficiency rather than a disciplinary event. They
have some experience with more serious offenses such as
fighting among students, students swearing at teachers,

stealing, gambling, and using alcoholic beverages and drugs. These things also happen in schools, but not often.

Some of these misbehavior activities are reported more frequently in senior high schools than in junior highs--cheating, making out, wandering in the halls, use of liquor and drugs, skipping school, kissing. Other misbehaviors are reportedly more commonly in junior high schools--fighting among students, stealing, assaulting a teacher(!), carrying firecrackers. Why this variation in behavior by age should occur is a subject for debate. It is often alleged that unruliness is common in junior high schools because it is the first encounter of most students with large institutions, because early adolescent years are characterized by so much physical and social change, and because students have not developed career expectations tied to their studies. Also, the students least interested in school are less likely to be present in senior high. By then some of the students who get into trouble in junior high will have dropped out.

Table 3-1 does show that three fairly serious offenses are reported "frequently" by substantial numbers of students and teachers--(1) truancy, (2) vandalizing school property, and (3) use of liquor or drugs. One third or fewer students and teachers think of committing a crime, carrying weapons, or assaults on teachers as frequent events. These data are worth attending, since many writers imply that crime and assault are everyday events. In these schools, they are not, according to both students and teachers. Yet, truancy, vandalism, and liquor/drug use--less deviant but still quite serious--are not uncommon. These problems are not things schools take lightly. Discipline problems may not be serious enough to provoke headlines, but they are clearly present if students and teachers believe truancy, vandalism, and liquor/drugs to be a frequent part of school life.

It is one thing to report impressions about behavior and another to have real frequency counts. As noted, simply because behavior is outrageous or remarkable, its frequency may be exaggerated. Thus, we ask how well the data in Table 3-1 are borne out by student and teacher reports about incidents in which they personally have been involved. On attendance violations, 26 percent of students said that they had skipped school sometime (that is, had been truant), about 19 percent during the current school year. Class cutting at least once was reported by 42 percent, 32 percent this year.[3] Much higher percentages of students in senior high schools both cut and skip, and among senior high school students twice as many say they have cut as that say they have skipped.

Students have said (Table 3-1) that there is a lot of truancy, although about three-quarters of them have never been truant. Truancy is a problem, if 26 percent of students are involved, but not an epidemic. Those who have skipped (been truant) this year say they have done so 2.5 times in the last year. Still, a few students said they had skipped 50 times in the last year.

Perhaps the behavior of some students is so well known that other students generalize in saying there is a lot of cutting and skipping. Whether these figures--32 percent cutting and almost 19 percent truant in a year--constitute a discipline crisis or not depends partly on point of view, of course. To many schools, having almost a fifth of pupils truant during a year may be intolerable. To others, there may be comfort in knowing that over four-fifths of the students have not been truant this year.

Attendance violations are not the only behaviors for which we can compare perceived frequency to actual committing of offenses. For vandalism and teacher assault, we can make similar comparisons. Whereas teachers report considerable vandalism (61.7 percent say vandalism takes place frequently or some of the time), about 31.5 percent of teachers have personally been involved with incidents they call vandalism. These figures may suggest that vandalism is more talked about than experienced.

Physical attack, perceived as fairly frequent by a third of teachers, has been personally experienced in the last three years by seven percent. Apparently, the seriousness of the offense affects perceptions of frequency. Although attacks on teachers may be endemic elsewhere, in these schools every sixteenth teacher has been physically attacked in the last three years. Interviews with teachers suggest that there are substantial differences among them in what constitutes a physical attack. Some consider a hallway altercation in which a teacher is pushed while breaking up a fight to constitute a physical attack. Others would not define the event that way.

There have been many questions about the reliability of the data on attacks on teachers. There are allegations that teachers are afraid to report attacks for fear administrators will perceive them to be partly at fault, and will punish rather than support them. Too it is alleged that teachers do not report attacks because nothing can be done about them in terms of compensation or redress. The data in this study, collected with anonymous questionnaires, do not raise the consideration of fear of administrators. They tell us that actual physical abuse is comparatively rare, although it is a subject of considerable concern for teachers. The National Safe Schools study results are similar to the incidence of physical assault--roughly one in two hundred teachers is attacked annually, according to that study.[4]

About 17 percent of teachers have been personally involved with a crime, about 48 percent with a prank or practical joke. Personal experience with verbal abuse is much more common--72.5 percent have been targets in the last three years. Again, the less serious problems of maintaining order and respect predominate.

We asked teachers to identify the most prevalent student behavior problems in the school, and their replies are shown in Table 3-2. It is lack of respect that teachers indicate most often as the common behavior problem, followed by truancy and disruptive behavior. Other behaviors identified

Table 3-2

Most Common Behavior Problems

In general, what would you say are the most prevalent student behavior problems in this school? (2 responses permitted)

Responses of Teachers	% of Responses
1. wandering, loitering	5.7
2. smoking	5.1
3. cheating	.6
4. throwing things	.6
5. lack of respect of teachers/students	20.9
6. drugs, alcohol	7.0
7. vandalism	5.1
8. talking in class	4.4
9. talking back	3.8
10. failure to perform academically	1.3
11. tardiness	.6
12. use of free time	1.3
13. "disrupting class," disruptive behavior	7.6
14. student apathy toward schools	2.5
15. unprepared for class	3.2
16. truancy and cutting	22.8
17. swearing	2.5
18. inattentiveness	3.8
19. lunch room offenses	1.3
N = 158	100.0

as prevalent also have to do with lack of respect (talking back, disruption of class, general attitude). Teachers seem quite uncomfortable with the general school behavioral climate.

The concern of teachers about lack of respect no doubt affects their morale. Dan Lortie has discussed at length how teachers obtain their rewards not from salaries, promotions, or professional collegiality, but from interpersonal relationships with students.[5] As teachers experience lack of respect, they lose the most meaningful rewards for their work. Lack of respect, however general or abstract it may seem, needs to be taken seriously as part of the complex of relationships between students and teachers.

The general pattern revealed by Table 3-2 is similar to that reported in a study of secondary schools in Maryland. The most common offenses reported by school principals were class disruptions, disobedience, insubordination, tardiness, smoking, fighting, truancy, class cutting, profanity, and verbal abuse. Such issues as weapons, drugs, gambling, vandalism, and assault were uncommon.[6] For the Marland schools, as for the schools in the study, insubordination-respect issues were major, and "real crime" was minor.

It is not easy, even for teachers, to get a good sense of the frequency of discipline and misbehavior problems. Teachers meet often and although admission of personal inadequacy in handling discipline problems may be awkward there are some discussions about them. In these discussions teachers may exaggerate or minimize events. In some instances teachers may not want to "back down" once they have reported an incident. They may be understandably reluctant to admit loss of temper or mishandling of an incident. Informal conversations, for obvious reasons, focus mostly on trouble spots.

Teachers may avoid discussions about discipline if they think there is disagreement about definition or practice. A teacher may feel that a given personal strategy usually works, but may be open to criticism for some reason. One high school teacher, for example, said he normally handled discipline problems by trying to embarrass the student. If a student were talking in class, the teacher would stop the class and go stand next to the offending student until the talking stopped. Or he might feign anger. Yet he was concerned that anger, particularly in a classroom setting, might disrupt the group unacceptably if used too often.

School student records, which might be the basis for more accurate data about misbehavior, are usually quite poor. What is entered in records very much depends on a set of largely uncontrolled factors: what definitions of misbehavior teachers have, what they report, whether discipline officers see the making of an entry on a record as appropriate, whether the offense is bargained down before it is recorded, etc.' There is good reason to doubt that most existing student records are much better as sources of data than the student-teacher grapevine. Many schools use card files for day-to-day matters and discard the boxes at the end of the year. Good records, routinely summarized, which might be useful for locating and analyzing problems, are not kept. Such records, if analyzed, might reduce the sense of threat and concern felt by teachers about school problems. But most schools have minimal discipline records.

Both teachers and students, then, generally lack any way of ascertaining with precision "what is going on." If the rumors begin to fly--about epidemic cheating or cutting--there is usually no way to confirm or stop them. A school, like the ones discussed here, with medium and low level discipline problems, does not have a very convincing way of denying that discipline is out of hand.

B. Responsibility for Control and Discretion

The way in which the discipline system is so bound up with other school activities is shown most dramatically when we turn to those who define and apply discipline. Studying what kinds of punishments occur, for what behaviors, is a good way to begin to understand the general climate of school behavior (and misbehavior). But it is in the enforcement system that the interconnectedness of discipline with the life of the school is most clearly demonstrated.

We turn in this section to the roles of teachers and administrators and how they feel about their activities. How do the pressures of the school setting constrain the disciplinary roles of teachers and administrators? And, above all, what are the characteristics of the kind of discipline that emerges from the patterning of relationships in schools?

The role of a teacher in the overall system of discipline is complex. First, there are classroom responsibilities. Within class the teacher is expected to foster learning, and usually that means some kind of structured situation for which order is presumed to be necessary. Absent unusual provocations, a teacher is expected to control classes without explicit backup. Teachers, of course, have varying views of the amount of order that is necessary for classroom effectiveness. One assistant principal said that many of the problems in the school were caused by teachers who sent kids out of the classroom because the teacher couldn't tolerate minor difficulties which, if allowed to pass, would

seldom recur. These teachers were overly rigid in their
limits. Moreover, many students pointed out that teachers
varied in their expectations as to class discipline. Some
teachers permit talking and fooling around, others do not.

If classes or individuals in classes cannot be controlled
as the teacher requires, principals and other administrators
may become involved in solving classroom-origin problems.
Individual students may be kicked out of class. "Go to the
office!" the teacher orders. But if many students are sent
to the office, or the same students are sent repeatedly, it is
difficult for the office to devise punishments which are
meaningful. The office as a place of punishment will not
work if it is used too frequently; it can cease to be a
significant threat.

Teachers are sometimes reluctant to refer students to
the office, lacking information about how the office handles
things. Or teachers may think that the office is not stern
enough. Teachers do not usually find out what happens to
the student who is sent to the office, for administrators are
not accustomed to reporting back to teachers. One teacher
commented on her feelings about using the office as a form
of discipline: "I don't want to be called a weak cookie, so I
don't send my problems down to the office until I really have
to." Another said, "I suppose _____ [the assistant
principal] knows what he is doing, but he and I don't agree
on the way to handle students, and I would rather not send
them there if I can handle things myself at all."

So, for within-class behaviors like talking out of turn,
cheating, sleeping, talking back, inattentiveness, and
swearing by students at other students, teachers expect to
handle the problems themselves. For any one of these six
problems, fewer than 20 percent of teachers say they would
turn to an outside person (see Table 3-3). They prefer to
handle problems themselves, if they can possibly do so.

Teacher responsibilities in the area of discipline are not
confined to the classroom. Teachers must become involved
in behavior in halls, cafeterias, even at extracurricular
events. In many situations outside the classroom, teachers
also usually try to handle things on their own.

In school, teachers indicated they would personally try
to handle students swearing at a teacher, excessive display
of affection among students, wandering, and inappropriate
appearance. More than half the teachers said they would
try to handle these problems themselves, or at least to take
the first step in handling the problem (Table 3-3). If additional measures were necessary, they might turn to others
for help, but they did not usually expect that any additional
help would be needed.

Table 3-3

Teacher Handling of Student Conduct Problems

What methods are you most likely to use? (in percents)

	Smoking in Prohibited Areas	Swearing at Teachers	False Fire Alarm	Wandering in Halls	Use of Liquor or Drugs	Truancy	Vandalism of School Property	Cutting	Throwing Things
Ignore	2.1	1.1	--	11.8	--	.6	--	--	6.2
Handle by self	24.1	57.3	2.3	67.4	6.1	19.0	6.7	36.6	35.9
Call parents or refer to principal	70.3	34.2	89.5	15.7	77.3	49.7	82.8	36.6	51.7
Refer to counselor	2.2	3.4	1.1	3.9	8.3	28.5	1.1	25.7	2.2
Recommend suspension	.5	.6	3.3	--	1.7	--	1.1	--	.6
Other	.5	3.3	4.0	1.1	6.7	2.3	8.3	1.1	3.4
TOTAL	99.7%	99.9%	100.0%	99.9%	100.1%	100.1%	100.0%	100.0%	100.0%
N =	182	178	181	178	181	179	180	175	175

For many other problems, however, only a small group of teachers would try to handle the matter personally-- smoking, fighting among students, fire alarm setting, theft, assault, liquor and drugs, truancy, vandalism, class cutting, carrying weapons, and criminal acts. For these things, teachers would automatically refer the behavior to the principal or someone else, rather than get involved. Teachers do not handle such problems, except in exceptional circumstances. For example, male teachers might try to stop a fight among students if it would be done with minimal personal risk.

In only a few problem situations do teachers suggest that a counselor might be the person to whom they would turn: truancy, cutting, inappropriate appearance, and excessive affection are problems for which teachers see some counselor role. Two of these problems are personal, and teachers may think of counselors as people with special sensitivity or links to students, having resources for the personal problem area but not generally able to do anything about discipline for problems of a different type.

An empirical study of teenage youth in Wisconsin, however, found that students generally held counselors in low regard, identifying them as attendance or discipline officers and not as sources of help or understanding.[8] In three of the schools in this study, counselors were in charge of attendance and late slips, types of activity having little to do with human relations. Counselors, as schools usually define their roles, are not an important part of a problem-prevention system. It is not surprising that teachers place as little reliance on them as they do. Teachers are somewhat likely to refer truancy and class cutting problems to counselors because they see counselors as attendance officers. This is the same perspective students hold.

Teachers obviously use discretion in defining, apprehending, and punishing misconduct. For some types of misbehavior in school, discretion is limited because school rules are quite clearly understood by all. As Table 3-3 indicates, for false fire alarms, nine out of ten teachers would refer to principals. For vandalism to school property and liquordrug and smoking violations, the rate of referral to the principal is also quite high.

Lines of responsibility for discipline are not, however, always clearly drawn or observed. Truancy, a serious offense, is not handled consistently, as shown in Table 3-3. Half the teachers would not involve the principal as the first step. This is the case even though these schools all have clear rules about truancy which call for reporting all offenders to the office. Similarly, class cutting may be handled in a variety of ways. The student who cuts is subject to differential treatment according to which teacher finds out. Some flexibility may be desirable and is certainly understandable, but the fact that truancy and cutting are handled so variably leaves both students and teachers unsure of the penalty. There are extra possibilities of misunderstanding, pressure, and lack of equity when such lack of agreement exists.

Because of the breadth of teacher responsibility in the discipline problem area, involvement for teachers with serious disciplinary measures is fairly common. One-third of the teachers in our study have been involved with in school suspensions, a punishment involving the assignment of students to a special room for a day. Most teachers have been involved with one or two internal suspensions a year, but one teacher reported participating in thirty. External suspensions are an even more common part of being a teacher. About 47 percent of the teachers said they had been involved with home suspensions, and one teacher said that he had been involved with 40 over a three-year period.

The roles of teachers, then, vary considerably in terms of the amount of discipline they apply. Some teachers want to handle many problems themselves, others are more likely to involve others on the school staff. The varying roles teachers choose are shaped by things such as their perception that administrators are too harsh (or easy), that students need responses tailor-made to their total school performance, or that they as faculty have special skills. Of course, an important dimension is how much misbehavior the teacher, with strongly developed ideas about order and autonomy, actually perceives. For example, a teacher who believes in maximizing student autonomy as part of the learning process may see nothing harmful in lots of low-level banter and friction, and consequently rarely be involved with enforcing rules.

As we have seen, for some kinds of problems teachers indicate a clear preference for handling things themselves. For other problems, like referring students to police or being a "judge" in discipline cases, teachers report that administrators bear the responsibility. Administrators usually contact parents of offending students, determine facts in "heavy" discipline cases, and handle emergency discipline problems.

There are some areas, however, in which teachers say they currently have the responsibility, and they would like to drop it. Overall, teachers are in agreement with the distribution of responsibility for discipline as it exists--with four exceptions. The four areas in which they want greater responsibility assumed by the school administration, and less by teachers, are rule enforcement (1) in the halls, (2) at extracurricular activities, (3) in the cafeteria, and (4) on the school grounds. These are all situations which are very unstructured and in which the teacher has few sanctions to bring to bear. Also, there is no way of fitting hall or cafeteria discipline into teachers' own professional images of themselves. Indeed, hall or cafeteria efforts to discipline may diminish classroom effectiveness.

In school systems throughout the country, administrators are, of course, aware of these trouble spots and of staff reluctance to become involved in policing. But few of them have been able to devise a satisfactory scheme for order or control that does not rely on teacher personnel. "Outsiders" for hall patrol have been suggested by some-- that is, outsiders who are community-based enforcement persons.[9] But having outsiders involved in school control raises other problems. Can a school reject the police, keep out unwanted community intervention, and still use non-professional outsiders for effective discipline? This is not an easy question, for the solution to one problem may cause other difficulties. Police liaison persons are permanent parts of some schools. Other schools have guards for the grounds. A few school districts have developed "principal support teams," usually groups of four who can be called upon for assistance at intense times. Paid support workers are sometimes used for lunchroom duty; teachers are sometimes paid extra for hall duty. A few schools are using student responsibility groups to diminish particular problems, such as vandalism.

What is important analytically is that the staff wishes to reduce its area of social control to the boundaries of the classroom. But the administration, which cannot control congregate areas with a skeleton crew, keeps the staff "on line," involving them in problems that sometimes challenge their competency. Inside their own classrooms, teachers acknowledge that they have different styles and tolerances, to which students must adjust. Individual styles, however, cannot last in the cafeteria, and the sometimes delicately balanced roles that teachers have established in their classrooms are called into question.

Teachers in our study were asked in what ways the types of behavior of other teachers contributed to student behavior problems. Only about five percent of teachers replied "none." The main teacher actions and attitudes that were identified as contributing to student misbehavior were not being strict enough (22.8 percent of responses), differential treatment of students (11.7 percent), and ignoring problems (7.6 percent). Also mentioned were lack of teaching ability, lack of respect for students, too much strictness, and failure to set a positive example. Teachers are not at all unified in viewing lack of strictness and lack of enforcement responsibility as key problems, but more teachers agreed on those points than on any other. What is probably most important is that teachers do hold other teachers responsible for discipline problems. Yet the faults they find with other teachers--lack of strictness and differential treatment--are part of the warp and weft of the learning institution.

Asked how behaviors of administrators contributed to student misbehavior problems, only six percent of the teachers said they did not. Administrators were criticized as being too easygoing or not strict enough (29.8 percent of responses), giving differential, nonuniform treatment to students (15.2 percent), and giving too many second chances (9.3 percent). A large number of other responses were also given. Teachers are much less likely to fault administrators for lack of concern with the problems of discipline than they are to fault other teachers. Some teachers are concerned about excessive administrator strictness and much use of fear rather than reason, but they are in the minority. Most teachers want the discipline regime tightened by other teachers and by the administration, yet most teachers saw no need to make changes in their own discipline methods.

The enforcement of school discipline is understandably spotty. It is bound up with teacher autonomy in classrooms and the lack of meaningful "joint" activity in administration-staff activities. Although teachers regard the disciplinary practices of others with some skepticism, they strongly favor the continuation of a discipline system which is "cellular" and therefore somewhat uncertain.

C. Punishments

Having discussed the prevalence of misbehavior in schools and the loosely structured system for responding to misbehavior, we turn in this section to punishment. First we examine student perceptions of what happens to rule violators. Then we discuss actual punishments and compare perceptions to the reality of punishments.

One important aspect of any system of regulation is what the people regulated perceive to be taken seriously and not so seriously by the regulator. The offenses identified by students as bringing lots of punishment are, in order, false alarms, assaults and crimes, liquor and drugs, vandalizing school property, stealing, carrying weapons, and swearing at a teacher, as shown in Table 3-4. Most of the behaviors perceived as involving some or lots of trouble are, according to both students and teachers, not frequent in schools. For example, assault is perceived as subject to considerable punishment and is, according to students, uncommon. Likewise punishment is perceived as modest or heavy for fighting, cheating, gambling, skipping school, and carrying firecrackers, and these behaviors are fairly infrequent. Students expect almost no sanctions for being unprepared, throwing things, kissing, swearing at other students, wandering, making out, and talking in class. Most of these behaviors are very common.

Although there is a general negative relationship between the extent to which students perceive that something

Table 3-4

Student Expectations of Consequences of Behavior

In your school would you get into a lot of trouble, some trouble, or no trouble for the following?

	Lot	Some	None	Total
Talking during class	2.8	71.2	26.0	100.0%
Fighting with other students	43.2	48.2	8.6	100.0
Swearing at a teacher	59.1	31.7	9.2	100.0
Cheating	37.0	53.9	9.1	100.0
Setting false alarms	84.9	6.1	9.0	100.0
Making out	8.9	30.3	60.8	100.0
Stealing	73.0	18.4	8.6	100.0
Wandering in halls	5.5	64.1	30.4	100.0
Gambling	36.3	46.0	17.8	100.1
Assaulting a teacher	80.8	10.9	8.3	100.0
Using liquor/drugs	76.6	14.5	8.8	99.9
Skipping	40.6	50.1	9.3	100.0
Vandalizing school property	75.5	16.9	7.6	100.0
Talking back to teacher	13.6	72.3	14.1	100.0
Possessing weapons	67.3	22.3	10.4	100.0
Carrying firecrackers	48.3	39.	12.5	100.0
Committing a crime	80.9	10.5	8.6	100.0
Swearing at other students	4.5	44.2	51.3	100.0
Kissing	4.1	24.1	71.8	100.0
Throwing things	7.1	74.7	18.2	100.0
Being unprepared	3.1	61.7	35.2	100.0

N = 1316

will get them in trouble and the extent to which they say it happens, the fit is not perfect. Some activities with heavy consequences (swearing at teachers) take place anyhow; thus the potential for punishment does not always serve as a deterrent. Overall, however, student reports of misbehavior and severity of punishment conform to the usual expectation that the more serious misbehaviors will have the most consequences. Both utilitarian deterrence and internalization of norms seem to be operative.

There is reason to be concerned about the fact that from five to ten percent of students think no trouble would result from assaulting a teacher, committing a crime, or possessing weapons. It is unlikely that any of these activities would be tolerated, and it seems likely that students recognize them as off limits. Perhaps the factor influencing the perceived likelihood of getting into trouble for this small percentage of students is the lack of expectation of being caught.

For almost all events, there is good reason for students to think they can "get away with it." According to the students who said they cut a class in the current school year, only 28.8 percent were caught. A similarly small percentage (32.1 percent) of those who skipped were caught. Moreover, penalties for cutting and skipping were often negligible. Of those caught for cutting, 19 percent said nothing happened, 28.7 percent had a mild penalty like a reprimand slip, being sent to the office, or being given a detention. To put it another way, of the 409 students who cut this year, 47 received a fairly harsh punishment, 43 had a milder punishment, and the rest were not punished at all. There is good reason for students not to be too apprehensive, then, about severe punishment. Students who know the system best--repeat rule breakers--are more informed about the likelihood of apprehension, drawing on their experience as a guide. Other students presumably see rule breaking occur and know there is often no real punishment. All in all, there is not much deterrence in school rule systems.

Once a student is apprehended for a rule violation, different penalties might result. Suspension, being kicked out of class, detentions, and a stern lecture are all possibilities. Or there may be no penalty. Punishments such as being suspended from school are reported by fairly small percentages of students (see Table 3-5). Even allowing for lapses in detection and enforcement, this seems to suggest that serious offenses are not common in these schools. Yet 25.7 percent of students have at some time been kicked out of class, a much larger number. Very nearly the same percentages of students are kicked out of class in junior and senior high schools.

Although sending students to the office is an easy, quick punishment, there are limits on the extent to which teachers can kick students out of class. One principal who was interviewed indicated he was likely to react negatively if a teacher sent student after student to the office. Teachers too have their own reasons for not kicking students out.

Table 3-5

Frequency of Punishments

Percent of students ever suspended: 8.2
   Median times suspended this year (for those ever suspended): 1.3
   Average times suspended this year (for those ever suspended): 1.6

Percent of students ever kicked out of class: 25.7
   Median times kicked out this year (for those ever kicked out): 1.4
   Average times kicked out this year (for those ever kicked out): 2.9

One teacher said that although she had the possibility of plenty of help from the principal, she sent students to him very infrequently. She referred a student to the principal only if in-class oral correction and private conferences in the hall or after class had failed. Only four of her students had been sent out all year, although some of them had been sent out several times, she said. She expressed pride in handling "her own problems."

Detentions are an alternate penalty, a disciplinary device used more widely than sending students to the principal's office. They are more informal, to both the teacher and the student. Over 36 percent of the student sample reported receiving a detention in the last five months. One student reported 60 detentions. Detentions are given very frequently in some schools, especially junior highs, hardly at all in high schools. Students who receive detentions may report to a central after-school facility, or stay with teachers in their individual classrooms. The types of incidents leading to detentions are shown in Table 3-6. Detentions are a mild form of punishment applied to rather low-level infractions, both in class and outside class. They may be the penalty for being sent to the office. In Middle City detentions are usually initiated by an assistant principal upon referral of a teacher. Formal detention records are not kept, and parents are not informed, though "informal" card file records may be kept on which detentions are recorded.

Table 3-6

Reasons Students Were Given Detentions

Briefly explain how you got the last detention (2 responses possible).

Reason	Percent of Responses
Talking in class	23.3
Tardiness	19.2
Incomplete assignment	6.1
Disruptive behavior	4.3
Gum chewing	3.3
Cutting class	3.3
Roaming	3.1
Talking back	2.6
Fighting	2.6
Other offenses	32.2
	100.0

N = 391

For more serious misbehavior, suspensions are more often the penalty.[10] In-school and home suspensions are both used in these schools, but for different purposes. In-school suspensions involve time spent in semi-isolation within the building and are not accompanied by parent notification. Only the principal or assistant principal can arrange in-school suspensions, and the in-school suspension room is generally supervised by an administrator. Indeed, in-school suspension may mean that the student sits in the principal's office or outer office for the set time. Counselors' offices may be used for in-school suspension purposes as well.

Teachers indicated that the principal purpose of internal suspensions was to punish inappropriate behavior (such as student disruption of class) or to cope with repeat offenders. Thus, in-school suspension was not considered appropriate for drugs and liquor, theft, or other more serious offenses. Internal suspensions were mostly for repeated low-level misbehaviors, or to provide cooling off periods for the parties involved.

Teachers were generally supportive of in-school suspensions, stating that they had a useful role in school management. One junior high school guidance counselor commented that in-school suspension was an effective deterrent to misbehavior, because students found it so extremely boring. Sitting in an office for the full school day without benefit of peer interaction was painful enough to deter misbehavior, she reasoned. As testimony to its effectiveness, students in Rural Place referred to the in-school suspension room as "the hole."

In-school suspensions have become more commonplace in the last decade and more elaborate. In-school suspensions offer the possibility of imposing sanctions without involving parents and without sending the student out of school on his or her own. They do not, so far, require due process hearings or other procedural considerations.[11] They may or may not appear on student records, and often they are not part of the required reporting to central school administration.

Out-of-school suspension, which happened to 8.2 percent of students, is made of sterner stuff. Observance of due process standards outlined in court decisions and state statute in Wisconsin requires that a student being given a home suspension have a statement of reasons why the suspension is taking place and the opportunity to tell his side of the story if he denies the charges. It is thus a bit harder to suspend students from school than to keep them in school for suspension.

The reasons for home suspensions received by students are shown in Table 3-7. Most of the offenses which led to home suspension are minor. These data on reasons for suspension are similar to those reported in other studies.[12] It is striking that the harshest penalty schools can administer is used mostly for modest offenses. This is another indicator of the paucity of serious discipline problems within the school.

Although there is little agreement about the purpose or utility of home suspensions, they are the harshest penalty the school is likely to use. Expulsion has virtually ceased in most school systems. Perhaps one student per decade is expelled in Middle City. State statutes and state education department rules outline extensive student protections and school board limitations on expulsion.[13] The student must repeatedly violate school rules or be endangering the health, safety, or property of others. The student and parents must receive a timely notice of a hearing before the local school board, with a statement of specific charges. Counsel may represent the student or parents and written minutes of the hearing must be kept. Witnesses and cross-examination are required should the school board decide to expel.   After the hearing the board must send its written decision to the parents and student.   Appeal to the State Superintendent of Public Instruction and then to the Circuit Court is possible.

Table 3-7

Reasons for Home Suspension

Why you were suspended the last time?

Offense	Percent of Responses
Smoking	34.3
Throwing things (snowballs)	10.4
Skipping/cutting	13.5
Liquor/drugs	6.7
False accusation	3.3
Swearing at pupils or teachers	3.3
Fighting	3.3
Other	25.2
	100.0

N = 96

With expulsion so formalized, the alternative of exemption (or early withdrawal) has been utilized more.   Student and parents may agree with the school that a student over 16 years of age is to be finally withdrawn, for "good cause," and then sign an "exemption form."   Parents may agree to this rather than go through the expulsion process, with the hope that the student can more easily attend a different school if withdrawal appears voluntary.   Of course, they may agree because they think the best interests of the child are not to continue in the school.[14]   From the school's perspective, exemption is a way of encouraging the student to drop out.

We find that about half the students in the sample say they have never received a punishment.   They may have misbehaved and not been caught—or caught and not punished—but they have been little involved with punishment for disciplinary infractions.   Isolated events involving violence or lawbreaking may occur, but most punishments are meted out for relatively minor infractions or for an accumulation of minor offenses, and most of the punishments are not onerous.

D.   The Rural Dimension--How It Differs

The data reported above were drawn from Middle City, an urban school setting with four thousand junior and senior high school students.   Our study replicated the survey-interview-observation approach in Rural Place, which had one school for grades 7-12.   Although our basic interest was in whether misbehaviors and penalties varied, we were also concerned with whether discipline played a different part in school life.   In a smaller rural school with students from backgrounds emphasizing more homogeneous values there should, according to social science hypotheses, be less misbehavior and less punishment.   Informal controls would operate to create fewer discipline problems and a less formalized discipline system.

These hypotheses were not sustained.   According to student responses in Rural Place, 52.8 percent cut class and 32.8 percent skipped school in the first six months of the school year.   These figures are higher than the urban ones. About 23.3 percent of the rural students said they had been kicked out of class (similar to the urban level), 21.2 percent had been given detentions, and 13.4 percent had been suspended (compared to 8.2 percent).   The reasons for being sent to the office or being given a detention were essentially the same for the rural and urban school systems.   But in the rural school, suspension more often resulted from liquor-drugs or fighting rather than smoking.   Rural Place suspension, used for more serious offenses, was mainly for removing disruptive students.

Rural school teachers and students report more everyday rudeness and upset, but see less serious misbehavior. Rural students and teachers thought some things (fighting among students, swearing at teachers, cheating, false fire alarms, and throwing things) more common than urban school groups, but committing a crime, carrying weapons, gambling, vandalism, and attacks on teachers were thought to be less common.   Teachers in rural schools, however, report more personal experience with vandalism and criminal actions (theft, extortion, etc.) but no personal physical attack. Internal suspension involvement for teachers is twice as common in the rural school, and almost seventy percent of teachers have been involved with external suspensions.

Though these data suggest some urban/rural differences, the striking finding is the similarity between the different school situations.   There may be less strong violence in rural areas, but there may be more "light violence" and abuse.   The rustic haven of the rural school free from problems, then, exists in the imagination or an earlier era. Informal systems or community standards do not operate to prevent misbehavior and make punishment unnecessary. Rural Place, like Middle City, had a full armature of rules and consequences, problems between staff and administration about expectations, and sizable numbers of students refusing to acknowledge the lines drawn by adults.

E. Conclusion

The data in this chapter reveal a discipline pattern with many not-very-serious infractions. There are frequent little incidents and a fair number of semiserious challenges, but it is believed by students and teachers alike that serious discipline events are uncommon. Certainly, there is rule breaking and misbehavior, but few of these represent a genuine overt sense of danger to students or teachers. Responding to this moderate level of misbehavior, the schools suspend a small percentage of students, but more commonly use more modest punishment. They kick students out of class or give detentions to deal with "everyday" offenses. The number of actions permanently separating student from school is very small. Although the schools have some order-keeping problems (particularly truancy), they do not seem to be obsessed with order or handicapped by its absence.

The data indicate that offenders are usually not punished (at least not for cutting and skipping), and if they are punished, half are lightly punished, only half seriously. The unpredictability of the punishment system stems directly from the discretionary handling of discipline in schools--teachers have enormous discretion as to whether they see, define, and punish an offense. There is little agreed strategy for handling situations that are not dire. For false fire alarms, teachers uniformly turn to the administration. But for many other misbehaviors, they handle the matters themselves, according to their own opinions of what is suitable and educational. The result, of course, is a tremendously varied set of outcomes for offenses--sometimes the teacher seems not to see anything happening and another time, the student is on the way to the office. However uncomfortable some teachers feel with the laxity of their peers, they prefer to retain the system which permits a great deal of professional latitude in handling problems and to strengthen only modestly the role of the administration in discipline. The extant system permits them considerable autonomy. The discretionary nature of discipline is, of course, familiar to teachers, and they seem to indicate that it brings results acceptable to them. Students may lack respect or carry on social visits in class, but teachers

believe they can cope under the prevailing discretionary
system with most of the problems that are raised.

Finally, the teachers, like the students, are probably
unaware of the amount of discretion in the system. Ironical-
ly, the system they wish to preserve is one in which punishment is quite occasional and trivial, as well as unpredictable. Given the low level of serious disciplinary challenge
to the school as an organization with educational goals, this
system with its slippage and discretion seems to function
reasonably well for the participants. Disciplinary activity
for the most part is embedded in the dynamics of school life.
Administrators and teachers share--increasingly--in the
responsibilities, and the ways in which they carry out their
tasks are conditioned by their relationships on a score of
issues. Curiously, the autonomy teachers have with regard
for discipline matters seems to work out in a general way to
provide the students, too with a great deal of fluidity.

NOTES

[1] These findings are similar to those reported by Daniel
L. Duke and Cheryl Terry, "What Happened to the High
School Discipline Crisis?" Urban Education 14 (1979).

[2] The list of discipline-evoking events was developed by
studying pretest student responses as to why students had
been kicked out of class, given detentions, or suspended.

[3] Since these data were collected halfway through the
school year, it can be argued that annual rates of truancy
and class cutting are understated. It might be that twice as
many people would cut/skip by the end of the year, or that
those who had already cut and skipped would simply do
twice as much. Given the high percentage of repeat offenders, detailed in Chapter 4, the latter interpretation seems
reasonable.

[4] National Institute of Education, Violent Schools--Safe
Schools (Washington, 1977). Also see Jerry J. Bellon, "A
Study of School Discipline in Tennessee," Report by the
College of Education, University of Tennessee, 1979.

[5] Dan C. Lortie, Schoolteacher: A Sociological Study
(Chicago: University of Chicago Press, 1975).

[6]Maryland Association of Secondary School Principals, "Final Report of the Task Force on Educational Programs for Disruptive Youth," Maryland Department of Education, 1976.

[7]Don Hermanson, "School Discipline--What the Discipline Records Tell Us," staff paper for Center for Public Representation, Madison, Wisconsin (March, 1977); Henry S. Lufler, Jr. "Discipline: A New Look at an Old Problem," Phi Delta Kappan 59 (February, 1978); Monika Wittig, "Client Control and Organizational Dominance: The School, Its Students, and Their Parents," Social Problems 24 (1976).

[8]Brown County Youth Resources Council, Brown County Study on Children and Youth Services, Volumes I and II, Green Bay, Wisconsin (1976).

[9]Alan Edward Guskin and Samuel Lorris Guskin, A Social Psychology of Education (Reading, Massachusetts: Addison-Wesley Publishing Co., 1970). There are also suggestions for special parole officers in schools, drawn from the regular teaching staff. Many programs for using outsiders in school have delinquency prevention as their main purpose, rather than alternative discipline systems.

[10]See Chapter 5 for a close analysis of suspensions.

[11]See the remarks of Professor Junious Williams in National Institute of Education, Conference Report on School Alternatives to Suspensions, Antoine M. Garibaldi (ed.), Washington, D.C. (1979).

[12]Children's Defense Fund, Children Out of School (Washington Research Project, Inc., 1974); Children Out of School in Ohio (Columbus: Citizens' Council for Ohio Schools, 1977).

[13]"Student Rights in Wisconsin Public Elementary and Secondary Schools", Wisconsin Department of Public Instruction, Madison, Wisconsin (September, 1977). This pamphlet includes clear guidelines on expulsion, suspension and corporal punishment. The Wisconsin guidelines in these areas are clearer than those in many states.

[14]Exemptions are also permitted for a short time for students needing personal counseling or personal support in order to continue in school. Exemption does not relieve the school district of obligations to supply continuing education. The vast majority of American states have provisions in their mandatory school attendance regulations whereby students

may be withdrawn "for good cause." Neither the procedure
nor the cause is specified.   See Ellen Jane Hollingsworth,
"Fairness and Discretion: Exemptions in Wisconsin," Report
to the National Institute of Education (Madison: Center for
Public Representation, 1981).

Chapter 4

FAIRNESS AND DISCRETION IN SCHOOLS

A teacher supervising a study hall was hit on the head by a thrown pencil. The teacher did not see the person who threw the pencil, but she did know the part of the room that it came from. The incident was brought to the assistant principal's [Mr. A] attention. He considered it serious, and determined to find the culprit. Mr. A had a student who had been sitting in the part of the room that the pencil came from brought in. Mr. A asked him if he did it. The boy denied throwing the pencil. He also denied knowing who threw it. Mr. A asked him if he was sure that he didn't know who did it. The boy stood on his denial.

Mr. A told the boy that he didn't think that he did it, but that it was difficult to believe that he didn't know who did, since he was sitting in the part of the room that the pencil was thrown from. Mr. A told the boy to try to remember what had happened, because the matter was serious. He advised the student to stop by his office before he went home to discuss the incident again.

The boy was obviously intimidated by the interrogation. He only spoke when he was asked a question and looked worried.

A second boy was then brought in by Mr. A. He did not seem at all intimidated. Unlike the first boy, he had been in trouble many times.

When Mr. A mentioned the pencil-throwing incident, he said that he was out of the room when the pencil was thrown. When asked if he had heard who had done it, he responded that the students were saying that "Animal" (the nickname of the first student) did it.

He talked openly, and did not seem to fear retribution. He promptly turned the conversation to a problem that he was having in obtaining a free lunch. He wanted Mr. A to help him and was very assertive.

Mr. A later found the pencil thrower. Further investigation led him to a student who witnessed the incident and told Mr. A who did it (it wasn't "Animal"). When this student was confronted he admitted to throwing the pencil, but stated that it hit the teacher inadvertently as it was thrown at another student. Despite this explanation, the student was suspended.

Mr. A said that he felt badly that he had pressured "Animal" so hard, as it turned out that he did not do it and may not have known who did. He said that he apologized to "Animal."

Discipline is a part of everyday life in schools, taking its shape from the kinds of relationships that exist among students, teachers, other school staff, and administrators. Although there is a formal and identifiable discipline system with rules and punishments, much of discipline is not so visible. Much of it takes place in classrooms and varies with the style of the teacher. Much of it is not written down or observed uniformly.

This discretionary system of discipline has evolved mainly as the result of the structuring of the school, not as the consequence of carefully thought through or agreed policy. In a general way we recognize that the way schools are organized stems from our conception that schools are expected to conduct a wide variety of education-related tasks and not to be concerned solely with academic skills. Thus, teachers must be instructors, counselors, club sponsors, chaperones, and hall guards. Given the multiplicity of roles expected of teachers in a modern secondary school (which often have quite heterogeneous student bodies), it is no wonder that a fairly fluid kind of discipline system has emerged. Indeed, that teachers vary in their use of discipline is so much a part of American education that any alternate system seems unthinkable. A discipline system with a great deal of discretion seems an almost necessary outcome of the expectations American society places on schools. This does not mean, however, that discretion, once understood, should be accepted uncritically. Even if discretion has subtle or hidden benefits, it may also have not-so-obvious costs.

The most troubling thing about discretion, especially in the human services, is the possibility that it will lead to considerable unfairness. Discretion, uncontrolled, is capable of abusing clients (in this case, students). On the other hand, for some students discretion may result in many benefits. They may be able to cut classes and wander the halls without being noticed, to swear cruelly at other students, or to break rule after rule without remonstrance because so much discretion is involved in discipline. At some point, then, the discretionary system of school discipline becomes unfair.

"Fairness" in schools is a troubling term because it is so general. Our use of it is limited to the following:

(1) Perceptions of fairness. Whether people (in this study, students) think that a system or institution is fair.

(2) Participation and Efficacy. Whether people (again, students) feel that they can have an effect on their institution, and whether they do have an effect.

(3) Nondiscrimination. Whether students and teachers think that certain groups are treated differently and whether they are in fact treated differently. Most attention is paid to this topic because fairness in the sense of evenhandedness, or nondiscrimination, is probably the most deeply rooted of our conceptions of what is "fair." If there is discrimination, does it proceed from ascribed status characteristics or from achieved characteristics?

As was the case with Chapter 2, even if the most prominent conclusions of this chapter follow expected sociological patterns, they may defy easy interpretation. What percentage of students' opinion will suffice to certify a system as fair? How much weight, in assessing fairness, should be given to opinions and attitudes and how much to behavior?

One useful way of looking at fairness is to assess whether the school's choices with regard to order and autonomy have appropriate consequences of fairness for most students. Great emphasis on order, for example, might be unfair in that students actively resented the rules, thought they could not change them and made no efforts. The rules might be a major subject of concern even though they were administered uniformly and without discrimination. Students might, in such a school, think the rules were very unfair because they had no input, and act out as a form of protest. A school maximizing autonomy, for purposes of contrast, might be much fairer, but not orderly enough to facilitate learning. Fairness, then, should be one of the major characteristics by which school discipline is assessed, but with the recognition that the functioning of the organization requires some limits on fairness.

A. Perceptions of Fairness

Although there are many ways of measuring fairness, we begin with attitudinal dimensions. Most students in our study think teachers treat students fairly all or most of the time (see Table 4-1), with more sense of fairness expressed in the senior high schools than in junior high schools (76.3 to 60.0 percent). The principal is usually perceived as fair, but teachers get even higher ratings for fairness. Principals in senior high schools were given better ratings than those in junior high schools.

Table 4-1

Perception of Fairness by Students

Are students treated fairly by:	Teachers	Principals
all or most of the time	68.6%	63.8%
sometimes	25.4	26.7
rarely or never	6.0	9.5
	100.0%	100.0%

Are teachers treated fairly by students?

all or most of the time	41.4%	
sometimes	45.6	
rarely or never	13.0	
	100.0%	

N = 1295

Interviews with students support the survey results very strongly. One high school junior said he felt students could expect teachers and guidance counselors to deal fairly with them and that rules (aside from the prohibition against card playing in lounge areas) were fair. Another, a student council leader, commented that, overall, teachers were open-minded and tried to communicate with students, treating them fairly: "I think most teachers try to understand us, and to be fair. You can talk to most of them pretty freely." Other students indicated that locker searches for drugs, detentions for throwing food, and other specific penalties were fair--if not always useful as deterrents.[1] There is a substantial dissent from this majority position, however. About one-third of students report teacher fairness only sometimes or less often.

Students see other students as being quite a bit more unfair than teachers or principals. Fewer than half thought students were fair to teachers all or most of the time. In common with other assessments, junior high students perceive more unfairness[2] on the part of their peers than do high school students. These findings cannot be explained exclusively in terms of having a lower opinion about those one knows best; if so, teachers would be seen as less fair than more distant principals.

There are two competing explanations for the greater unfairness perceived by students in junior high schools:

(1)   Junior high schools allow less autonomy. They have more questionable rules; dropping out is difficult, except for those few who sign "exemption" forms; elective courses are fewer; personal freedom is less (smoking, for example, is commonly prohibited in junior high schools but sometimes accepted in senior high schools); and junior high students are less likely to be granted "adult" status.

(2)   Junior high schools have more misbehavior and punishment. The isolation and concentration of preadolescents exacerbate natural egocentrism and other "normal pathologies" of that developmental stage. Yet overall, misbehavior is not more frequent nor punishment more severe or inaccurate according to the data gathered in this study.

Our data suggest that lack of autonomy in junior high schools is more likely to be the source of perceptions of unfairness in junior high schools. Overall there is not more misbehavior in junior highs, nor more punishment, so it is unlikely that students are responding to a reign of terror when they report more unfairness.

Other studies have shown significant and consistent, if small, relationships between measures of fairness and student misbehavior/ crime.[3] Our data show the same links. The greater the extent to which students think the administrators and teachers within the system are fair, the less likely they are to cut, skip, be kicked out of class, etc (see Table 4-2).[4] The causal relationship, if any, could run in various directions. Students who have been disciplined might have been treated unfairly or simply be expressing resentment about a just punishment, or misbehaving students may have a higher level of alienation from the school.[5]

Table 4-2

Relationship Between Fairness and Misbehavior*

Student sense of fairness**		Cut	Skip	Kicked Out	Given Detention	Suspended
HIGH	3	39.9%	20.7%	18.7%	25.7%	4.6%
	2	35.6%	23.3%	20.7%	33.1%	6.2%
	1	47.1%	26.6%	30.6%	44.9%	11.5%
LOW	0	49.2%	39.5%	42.1%	49.2%	13.4%

N = 1295

*Significant at the .001 level.
**The sense of fairness scale measures number of "all or mostly fair" responses a student gave regarding principals, teachers, and other students.

B.   Participation and Efficacy:
Can Students Change the Schools?

One response of students to perceptions of unfairness would be for them to try to change the practices they find offensive. Existing research has pointed out the willingness of many students to become involved with changes in the expressive area, but the lack of interest in more instrumental changes. Thus, for free speech, short skirts, and hair styles, mobilization among students was fairly easy to achieve. For instrumental and long-term changes such as faculty recruitment and salaries or curriculum planning, even in environments welcoming and wanting student input, it has been difficult to achieve student involvement.[6] These instrumental changes, of course, require much more time and are not "settled" quickly or for good.

Students in the schools we studied indicated consider-able confidence that they could do something to affect many types of school activity (see Table 4-3). Relative to disci-pline types of issues (the first six listed in the table), between 47 and 73 percent thought something could be done, at least sometimes. Smoking was the area most resistant to change, due in large measure to a firm school board policy against smoking in Middle City junior high schools. Smoking was one of the few offenses, other than truancy, which had received any attention from policy-makers in the community. It was not left to the individual schools to decide policy. Both smoking and throwing snowballs were to result in auto-matic suspension of the offender in Middle City junior high schools. Policies were different in the high schools.

Students in general felt more able to affect nondisci-pline issues (the last six in Table 4-3), but the differences between feelings of efficacy in changing discipline and non-discipline areas are fairly small. Students think they can change things or at least change some things. The very fact that so many students think discipline practices are open to change is a kind of fairness measure to begin with,

Table 4-3

Changing the School

Do you think students can do anything to change the way the school is run in any of the following areas: (percent responding always or sometimes)

Hall privileges	72.8
Disciplinary procedures	59.5
Punishment by teachers	57.8
Classroom rules	71.4
Rules about smoking	47.2
School rules in general	67.1
Homework	61.0
Grades	63.6
Textbooks	54.8
Class schedules	76.9
After-school activities	87.4
Dress rules	72.9

N=1290

but whether they have exercised the option which they perceive is another question.

Most students (70.7 percent) have never tried to make
a change in any of the areas listed in Table 4-3.   Differences between junior and senior high school respondents in
terms of attempting change are trivial.   Only a minority of
students have tried to make changes in any area, and most
of the attempted changes did not pertain to discipline.
Referring to discipline, of the hundreds of students surveyed, 24 had tried to change hall privileges, 25 had tried
to change classroom rules, 34 had tried to change smoking
rules, 26 had tried to change teacher behavior, 35 to change
the student code.   Other changes were sought by even
fewer students.   In all, only 2-3 percent of students had
tried to challenge any discipline-related area.   More students
had challenged two nondiscipline issues--grades (62) and
class schedules (61)--but even these numbers are small.

In confronting these data one wonders why students are
so little involved in change efforts.   Perhaps students are so
overwhelmed by the system, and so little rewarded when
they try to change it, that absence of effort is the rational
choice.   Students trying to change things are so unlikely to
succeed that their selective preference for no activity may
be rational.   Unfortunately (for our understanding), another
inference is also plausible: although students think that
they can be efficacious if they wish, they believe that the
system is so fair that they do not try to make changes.
Interview data support the presence of both perspectives
among the student population.   Some students also felt that
schools were special institutions which could not be "fair" in
the sense that other institutions or organizations might be
expected to be fair.   Schools under the circumstances were
not so unfair.   Finally, about a third of the students have
said schools are not fair places.   To those students, there is
an additional reason not to get involved in changing the
school, since one may be punished unfairly for one's efforts.

Students' Understanding of Their Legal Rights.
Another side to a sense of efficacy is the extent to which
individuals understand their rights under law.   Students are
not well informed about certain basic legal rights in the area
of discipline.   They seriously misunderstood the protections
available to them under court decisions and statutes. As part
of the survey, students were asked to indicate whether each
of the eleven statements shown in Table 4-4 was true or
false.   They could also say "not sure."   On only two questions did a majority of the students--a small majority--give
the correct reply.   More students knew about privacy rights
of school records, an item often included in school codes,
than about any other issue.   They also know about the right

Table 4-4

Student Information About Legal Rights Involving Discipline

	% Giving Correct Response	Correct Response
1. If a student's rights are violated, individual administrators and school board members can be sued.	28	T
2. A student can be suspended or expelled for skipping school.	11	F
3. A student has the right to a hearing before being transferred to another school for disciplinary purposes.	54	T
4. Teachers can lower students' grades when they skip school.	31	F
5. If a student is suspended, the principal can require the student's parent(s) to come to school before the student is readmitted.	5	F
6. A student has the right to a hearing before a short suspension	27	T
7. Outsiders need your permission or that of your parents before they can see your records.	57	T
8. For teachers to hit students is illegal in Wisconsin.	18	F
9. Under some circumstances, even a teacher can expel a student from school.	45	F
10. A student has a right to a lawyer if he or she is about to be suspended.	28	F
11. All schools in Wisconsin must have a Student Bill of Rights.	12	F

N = 1295

to have a hearing before disciplinary transfers take place. But as to hearings before suspensions and lowering of grades in response to truancy, they are in general not

acquainted with the Supreme Court rulings or the state
education agency guidelines.

Considering their serious lack of accurate information
about student rights, it is questionable how much reliance
for creating or maintaining procedural fairness should be
placed on students. It is true that the majority of students
say the system is fair, and that they could have some impact
on changing it. But they do not have a good sense of their
rights. Nor do they have records of having brought about
change. It is questionable whether they can assess fairness
related to rights they do not know they have.[7] Therefore,
we need to think carefully about the real meaning of student
fairness assessments. Overall, the majority of students have
feelings of fairness and efficacy. That such feelings exist
may be almost as important as whether they can be
substantiated.

C. Nondiscrimination in Discipline

We turn now to one of the most commonly accepted
senses of fairness--nondiscrimination. That people should
not be treated differently simply because they are members
of one or another group is a deeply imbedded value in our
culture. The matter is more complicated than this, however.
If people may not be treated differently as members of a
group, does it follow in all cases that they may be treated
according to their individual actions? Generally, we would
say the answer to this question depends on whether there is
a sound connection between the action and the differential
treatment. We argue that it would not be fair for students
with high grades to be punished less for the same offense,
although it is certainly fair to reward high grades; and if
students with high grades are punished less because they
are not repeat offenders, the statistical appearance of
unfairness may disappear on closer analysis. Another
complicating factor is that labeled individuals who are
punished justly for their actions may come to be perceived
and even to act as a group. Their early misfortune may
improperly influence later experiences in ways that are
extremely difficult to recognize and control (see Chapter 5
on "troubled students"). We examine, therefore, not just
the effects of ascribed status but of achievements and previous misbehavior as well as student experiences with school
discipline.

The discussion of differential treatment which follows
takes a variety of achieved, ascribed, and behavioral
statuses and analyses them in five categories: (1) general
student perceptions, (2) misbehavior (specifically cutting

and skipping), (3) being caught, (4) being punished, and (5) the male/female differential.

General Student Perceptions. Students were asked how many teachers applied rules differently depending on who the student was. About two-thirds (63.1 percent) of the students thought no or few teachers applied rules differentially, with slightly more confidence voiced in uniformity of treatment by junior high school students than by senior high students. How can we relate this to the other fairness responses reported? Junior high school students report more teacher unfairness, but junior high school students report less differential rule application. Senior high students report more variation in rule application and more fairness. These data, when linked, may suggest that senior high school students seem to find differential rule application (or discretion) generally fair. They accept the individual tailored penalty or treatment, the departure from uniformity as suitable. Junior high students find the system uniform and unfair.

Student and teacher respondents were both asked if students with various characteristics would be treated better, the same, or worse when they got into trouble. Their responses are shown in Table 4-5. Overall, students and teachers agree as to who gets differential treatment. But there is one divergence of note--students attach much more importance than teachers to having parents who are friends of the teacher in accounting for differences in treatment. We look later at the extent to which the perceptions in Table 4-5 are right.

By and large the ascribed characteristics students bring into the school are not perceived as a source of different treatment. Being rich, minority, poor, or male does not, students and teachers agree, have much to do with how you are treated if you get into trouble. It is what students do in school--grade and activity patterns, as well as trouble patterns--that is believed to cause different discipline treatment to be meted out. Both teachers and students agree that the labelling that goes on is not grossly based on characteristics of origin. If stereotypes of origin cause different treatment, it may be because they influence grades and trouble experience, which in turn cause different discipline treatment.

Overall, teachers tend to perceive more uniformity of treatment than students do. The average percentage of teachers identifying differential treatment for any reason is 35.7; for students the score is 43.5, somewhat higher. Teachers, then, see themselves as fairer and more uniform than students think they are. This is not very surprising,

Table 4-5

Teacher Variation in Treatment of Students

Would a student be treated differently (better or worse) if he/she were: (percent responding "YES")

	Teachers	Students
Rich	20.3	27.7
Not in school activities	32.3	37.7
Had a police record	52.7	69.4
Made top grades	68.0	83.1
Minority	6.0	14.1
Active in school activities	46.9	50.0
Parents are friends of teacher	35.8	64.2
Male	12.7	18.5
Poor	14.7	17.7
Female	16.7	21.7
Fooled around in class	73.1	81.4
Older	16.8	18.0
In trouble often	75.0	85.4
Younger	5.0	11.8
In trouble for the first time	45.6	42.3
Sports team member/cheerleader	50.0	52.2
N =	194	1290

in that most groups see themselves as more evenhanded than outsiders assess them to be. According to both groups the most different treatment would presumably accrue to a student with low grades who had been fooling around in class and had been in trouble often. These are the students who are believed to be most likely to get worse punishments, even when their offenses are the same as those without two strikes against them.

Tables 4-1 and 4-5 present the same dilemma of interpretation--whether the levels of unfairness indicated are serious. If 28 percent of students think wealth affects the way misbehaving students are treated, and teachers agree, how serious is the problem? If one-third of students think teachers and administrators are unfair, are schools unfair? These are debatable, difficult questions.

The general pattern observed in these various measures of fairness is that most students think there is fairness most of the time in the way students are treated, that discrimination and differential treatment are not commonplace at all. To the extent discrimination and differential treatment occur, they stem more from what the student does in school than from social standing.

Misbehavior (Cutting and Skipping). Let us look next at the way in which students with different ascribed and achieved characteristics report on their behavior patterns (Table 4-6). According to their own reports, those students with the following characteristics consistently did more cutting and skipping: trying to make changes in school, being older, making lower grades, having low class rank, coming from a lower family socioeconomic status, and not being an athlete or cheerleader. General school activity, sex, minority status, and student government roles are not consistently

Table 4-6

Differences in Skipping and Cutting
by Student Characteristics

Student Characteristics	Cutting	Skipping
1. older	24.0% more**	12.8% more**
2. white	11.4% more	4.2% more
3. father has professional, managerial job	12.4% less*	9.0% less*
4. high class rank	18.8% less**	18.9% less**
5. male	9.4% less**	3.4% more
6. involved with making changes at school	9.9% more*	8.6% more*
7. fairly active in school (one or more activities)	no difference	less
8. A, B, or AB average	15.8% less*	17.0% less**
9. athlete or cheerleader	15.6% less**	10.0% less**
10. student government participant	.2% more	9.5% less
N =	995	995

* $X^2_{.01}$ significant at the .01 level
** $X^2_{.001}$ significant at the .001 level

related to cutting and skipping as reported by students. Misbehavior (cutting and skipping) are, then, systematically related to age and family background (things beyond the student's control) and to some school activities and achievements. This pattern is consistent with literature which suggests that students with a strong sense of personal efficacy (especially older students) who are thwarted in their efforts to change schools turn to deviance in their frustration.[8]

Being Caught. In a truly just system all students who cut or skip are equally likely to be caught, regardless of their personal characteristics. Teachers and administrators should be equally likely to catch class-cutting students of any size, sex, or school demeanor. On the other hand, if there are widespread stereotypes about student behavior among teachers and other enforcers, then those stereotypes might influence the "rates of apprehension." For example, if teachers believe that those with low grades are more inclined to cut and skip, they might be "on the lookout" for students with low grades who are wandering the halls or leaving campus improperly. Those students would thus be caught more often for cutting and skipping. Teacher stereotypes about cutting and skipping students would cause them to pay less attention to high achievers if they were loitering or leaving the campus.

Table 4-7 shows that some bias exists as to who is caught for skipping and cutting. Some of this bias has a kind of reasonableness to it, in that from Table 4-6 we know what characteristics are consistently associated with cutting and skipping. Older students cut and skip more and are caught more. Evidently teachers are on the lookout for them. Students with lower grades, poor classwork, or more modest family backgrounds (three characteristics associated with cutting and skipping) are also caught more often. By and large then, the students whose characteristics are associated (rightly) with cutting and skipping are caught more often. The exception is that students who have tried to make changes in school, though they cut and skip more often, are not caught more often.

The disciplinary net, however, does not fall evenly on all who cut and skip. It does not respond directly and consistently to the actual characteristics of those who break the 16rules. For example, males cut less often, but are more likely to be caught. Males do skip more often, but are less likely to be caught for skipping. But there is a general sort of fit between the commission of misbehavior and its apprehension. That those who misbehave more are more likely to be caught seems both fair and unfair.

Table 4-7

Factors Affecting Being Caught

Were you ever caught?
(for those who cut and skipped)

Student Characteristics	Caught Cutting	Caught Skipping
1. older	11.9% more**	12.5% more
2. white	a	a
3. father has professional, managerial job	7.2% less	14.1% less
4. high class rank	17.8% less**	14.6% less
5. male	8.5% less	2.7% more
6. involved with making changes at school	2.7% less	1.4% less
7. fairly active in school	less	less
8. A, B, or AB average	20.5% less**	11.8% less
9. athlete or cheerleader	17.2% less**	9.6% less*
10. student government participant	15.0% less**	4.1% less
N =	381	225

a   numbers too small for reliable analysis
* X^2 .01 significant at the .01 level
** X^2 .001 significant at the .001 level

Punishment. Detection is, of course, just one step in
the discipline process. It does not, as we have seen, apply
equally to all groups according to their misbehavior. And,
as reported in Chapter 3, most who cut and skip are not
caught. But there is a further discretionary step when
someone is caught--to dismiss the offense or to exact some
punishment. The same issue arises here as in the previous
section: Once someone is caught for misbehaving, to what
extent should personal characteristics affect punishment?
Should punishments be more or less invariantly related to
misbehaviors (a kind of determinate sentencing)? Or should
they be applied with discretion, according to the characteristics of the apprehended?
    We asked students what happened the last time they
were caught for cutting or skipping. For most students,
penalties are light or nonexistent, but as Table 4-8 shows,
there is variation in the way students with different

characteristics fare. Those who are older, are male, have
high grades, or are athletes are punished less.

According to student reports, two groups which cut
less are caught and punished less--top students and
athletes. These groups benefit more than any others identified in this study from the discretionary nature of the discipline system. Males, to trace back through several tables,
cut less, are caught more, and are punished less if caught.
Older students cut much more and are caught more, but are
punished less. Those of higher socioeconomic status, though
they cut less and skip less and are caught less, are punished just as much as those of other status. We see, thus,
that the inconsistencies visible in apprehension / are also
present in punishment. The discipline system is not fair in
the sense of total consistency. The way discipline works is
mainly unpredictable, although some groups seem to benefit
consistently.

Table 4-8

Type of Punishment for Cutting by Student Characteristics
(if caught)*

Student Characteristic	Some Punishment**
1. older	13.9 less
2. white	***
3. father has professional, managerial job	.1 more
4. high class rank	8.3 less
5. male	15.4 less
6. involved with making changes at school	3.0 more
7. A, B, or AB average	19.5 less
8. athlete or cheerleader	19.5 less
N =	122

* numbers of students caught for skipping are too small for
analysis by severity of punishment
** rather than no punishment or offense dismissed
*** numbers too small for reliable analysis

The Male/Female Difference. One group that seems to
be punished more is the males. We have seen in Table 4-6

that males cut class less than females and skip only slightly more often than females. Yet the punishments of the school--being kicked out of class, being given detentions, being suspended--fall much more heavily on males.

If the violation patterns in cutting and skipping are presumed to be general, that is, if male behavior is only intermittently worse than female behavior, a lack of fairness in administration of punishment may exist. The data in Table 4-9 indicate that males are in general punished with being kicked out of class for the same things that get girls kicked out. Yet they are suspended for somewhat different activities (Table 4-10), activities which may seem more threatening to school order.[9] Girls may cut, and girls may smoke, but their conduct violations remain more within the schools' definition of tolerable, so they are not kicked out of class or given detentions, or suspended on the same scale.

Table 4-9

Reasons Students Were Kicked Out
of Class--Most Recent Event

	Male %	Female %
Class misbehavior, talking, out of seat	37.6	41.0
Disruptive behavior	20.2	17.1
Talking back or disobeying teacher	14.6	19.0
Throwing things	5.1	1.0
Liquor/drug use	1.1	---
Truancy	1.7	1.9
Tardiness	3.9	1.0
Other	15.7	19.0
TOTAL	99.9%	100.0%
N =	178	105

Fighting, throwing things, and using liquor are often mentioned in general society as types of behavior more typical of males--and, thus, might be reasons for the greater use of suspensions with males. These data, however, do not clearly support such generalizations, in that suspended females are about equally likely to have fights and to use drugs or alcohol.

Table 4-10

Reasons Students Were Suspended--Most Recent Event

	Male %	Female %
Smoking	29.8	42.1
Throwing things	15.8	--
Cutting class	14.0	13.2
Swearing at teacher, principal	1.8	5.3
Fighting	1.8	5.3
Drugs, alcohol	5.3	7.9
Other (for example, tardiness, false accusation, gambling, vandalism)	31.5	26.2
TOTAL	100.0%	100.0%
N =	57	38

     Other evidence suggests that within-school deviance
among girls tends to be of a quieter, less visible nature: it
is less threatening to others, less detected, and less punished.   One vice-principal commented that girls smoked and
skipped frequently, whereas boys fought, drove cars reck-
lessly around school, and were insubordinate.   He added
that boys created problems alone, girls tended to operate in
groups.   A boy commented that girls got into less trouble
for yelling in the halls, but that swearing by girls was less
accepted by teachers than swearing by boys.   There is some
fragmentary evidence that the responses to many discipline
problems raised by girls are to utilize counselors rather than
to use the penalty system.   Assistant principals are usually
male and may feel less comfortable about disciplining girls.[10]
     Teachers indicate that they often prefer conferences
and counseling to suspensions and detentions; such alternatives have a tone of human service about them.   If female
offenses are defined differently and are diverted into counseling whereas male infractions are handled through disciplinary actions noted in school records and involving
parents, there is need for school systems to consider the
fairness of such differentiation.   Certainly the lack of sex
bias in the incidence of cutting and skipping suggests that a
penalty system reflecting many more detentions and suspensions for males needs internal monitoring.   This problem

needs much more investigation, but on the surface it seems that males are probably not given equal treatment, considering their misbehavior.

D. Urban/Rural Fairness Differences

The rural school district in which comparable measures were obtained reflected considerably less student feeling of fairness. Whereas 59 percent of students thought teachers were fair, only 28.4 percent thought the principal was fair, and 35.7 percent thought students were fair. Only 43.8 percent of students said no or few teachers applied rules differently--a much smaller vote of confidence for faculty fairness than in the urban school system. On the items shown in Table 4-5, students and teachers both thought there was more "different treatment" than had been mentioned in the urban school system. For the most part students and teachers agreed that different treatment was related to making top grades, fooling around in class, and being in trouble often. Students thought having a police record or having parents who were friends of the teacher also resulted in different treatment; teachers disagreed. The rural school people, like the urban ones, thought variation in disciplinary sanction proceeded from achievement, or lack of it, within school.

Less sense of fairness is not, however, reflected in markedly different behavior patterns. Urban and rural schools may differ in fairness, but, as Chapter 3 has indicated, they differ little in misbehavior problems and sanctions.

In the rural school we found that the same sort of hit-and-miss patterns existed, except for good students. Whether a student was older or male or from a family with higher socioeconomic status did not systematically influence whether the student was caught and punished for misbehaviors such as cutting and skipping. Good students, however, did benefit uniformly, in that disciplinary sanctions were applied to them far less often when they misbehaved.

E. Conclusions

The schools are highly legitimated institutions, and a strong majority of students think that they are fair. But there is a sizable and troubling dissent. Students think that they can change the system, but they hardly ever try to do so or succeed when trying. Purely ascribed statuses such as wealth and race do not make much difference in the way students are treated, but are sufficiently powerful to suggest some need for change in current practices. More important is the way students are treated are the achieved statuses, the positive ones, such as grades and being an athlete, and the negative ones, such as having been in trouble before. Males and females are treated differently, but the differences are mediated through different ways of presenting misbehavior and a tendency for the schools to select "therapeutic" punishments for girls.

Analysis of these statuses is complicated. Such statuses clearly do not seem to be proper grounds for influencing or modifying disciplinary action, yet their influence may be very difficult to dissolve. In the highly decentralized, discretionary world of discipline, positively and negatively charged personal relationships take their toll.

Some of the perceptions and the findings in this study need extended inquiry. If "good students" are treated more favorably, we need a better sense of the opportunity the poor and minority students have to be good students.[11] In-school activities are probably related to nonschool factors. As Chapter 5 will indicate, teachers do not hesitate to explain serious school misbehaviors in terms of home background. Yet overall, as Table 4-5 shows, they claim that they do not consistently apply discipline differently because of pupils' characteristics or origin.[12]

Finally, we need to continue to focus on the relationship between teacher discretion in handling discipline problems and fair outcomes. In a school with dozens of teachers and classrooms, the overall flow of tasks is handled in a very decentralized way. The individual classroom teacher is the person setting the standards and, in most cases, deciding the program for the classroom. There is enormous discretionary control for the teacher in the substance of the teaching process, and to some extent in administrative activities as well. To what extent is it possible to increase fairness without invasion of desirable discretion? In some situations, there is no adequate reason to have discretion rather than rule, and in some situations in which discretion is desirable and necessary, its exercise may nevertheless be unfair.

Given the way the United States public schools are organized, it is obvious that discretion will remain a central aspect of day-to-day life.[13] Teachers, with ever-stronger professional organizations, will insist upon it. Administrators, wanting teachers who are both responsive and responsible, will move only small steps toward any curtailment in discretion. The issue becomes the best mix of fairness and discretion and not the exclusion of one or the other. Fairness can very likely increase markedly in many school environments without implications for diminishing meaningful discretion. Inasmuch as the discussions about increasing fairness are seen as threats to discretion, there cannot be much headway for fairness. Casting fairness in the context of the basic respect teachers want to foster, not in terms of antiteacher strategies, is more useful and meaningful.[14]

Another possibility for limiting discretion is to implement a more systematic structure of penalties. A more structured, graduated penalty system would remove some variation in punishment, but would really affect only repeaters (a rather small percentage of students). Some of the randomness of the penalties will be removed through systematization, but there is no cure for the fact that discipline officers may tend to watch some groups more attentively for errors, or to define certain behaviors differently.[15] In Great Britain minority groups which were alleged to cause more trouble and crime in schools were studied and found to commit fewer infractions. The minority was simply much more visible, much more easily labeled. There are various steps which may be meaningful in promoting fairness of treatment, but equality may not result so long as the intake for the discipline system is skewed because some groups are "watched more."

Perhaps teachers will reshape their observation patterns if they have good reason to think they are being unfair in their behavior. For example, if female students say they cut or skip more than male students, and teachers are aware of it, probably teachers would adjust their own enforcement behavior and boys would no longer report greater likelihood of being caught for offenses. Or, if teachers find that athletes and cheerleaders cut class and are truant on the same scale as others, they will probably be even less likely to give them special handling (negative or positive).

NOTES

[1]Carl Werthamn, "Delinquents in Schools: A Test for The Legitimacy of Authority," Berkeley Journal of Sociology 8 (1963).

[2]Richard P. Benoit, "An Investigation of Eighth Grade Student Attitudes Regarding Middle School Disciplinary Practices" (Ph.D. dissertation, Florida Atlantic University, 1975).

[3]James M. McPartland and Edward L. McDill, "The Unique Role of Schools in the Causes of Youthful Crime," Report 216, Center for Social Organization of Schools, Johns Hopkins University (1976).

[4]Throughout this book chi square tests of significance are used to indicate how likely it is that the relationships between two variables occur by chance. Many of the data are reported in terms of distributions, for which tests of significance are not applied.

[5]Arthur L. Stinchcombe, Rebellion in a High School (Chicago: Quadrangle, 1964).

[6]Center for New Schools, "Strengthening Alternative High Schools," Harvard Educational Review 42 (August, 1972).

[7]"Student Rights in Wisconsin Public Elementary and Secondary Schools," Wisconsin Department of Public Instruction, Madison, Wisconsin (1978).

[8]Christine Bennett and J. John Harris III, "Suspensions and Expulsions of Male and Black Students: A Study of the Causes of Disproportionality," Urban Education 16 (1982).

[9]Don Hermanson, "School Discipline: What the Discipline Records Tell Us," prepared for Center for Public Representation, Madison, Wisconsin (1977).

[10]Gary J. Jensen and Raymond Eve, "Sex Differences in Delinquency," Criminology 13 (1976).

[11]Christopher Jencks, Marshall Smith, Henry Acland, Mary Jo Bane, David Cohen, Herbert Gintis, Barbara Heyns, and Stephan Michelson, Inequality (Basic Books, 1972).

[12]Marilyn S. Baur, "Truancy: An Examination of Social Structural Influences and Traditional Approaches" (Ph.D. dissertation, University of Colorado, 1976). This study turns attention to the organizational, not personal, characteristics associated with truancy.

[13]Michael E. Manley-Casimir, "School Governance as Discretionary Justice," School Review 82 (1974).

[14]Ellen Jane Hollingsworth, "The Impact of Student Rights and Discipline Cases on Schools," Schools and the

Courts, Vol. II (Eugene, Oregon: Clearinghouse on Educational Management, 1979).

[15]Naomi F. Faust, Discipline and the Classroom Teacher (Port   Washington,   New   York: Kennikat   Press,   1977), Chapters 9 and 10, especially.

Chapter 5

TROUBLED STUDENTS, SCHOOLS, AND TEACHERS

A. Troublemakers

Those working in schools have shared perspectives on
the problems they face, perspectives at times well grounded
through analysis of a particular issue and sometimes unsupported by any analysis. Teachers and administrators in
Middle City and Rural Place felt that most discipline problems
could be attributed to a small group of students whom they
called "the troublemakers." These students were variously
described as being "the one percenters," "the five percenters," and so forth.[1] But regardless of the percentage
used, school personnel saw this small group as responsible
for causing most classroom disruptions and most out-of-class
vandalism.[2]

School personnel commonly held a number of assumptions about the nature of troublemakers and the role they
played in the schools. These assumptions included the following: groups of troublemakers present in a classroom or
school have a cumulative effect on discipline problems;
troublemakers could induce properly behaved students to join
them in rule-breaking; most troublemakers were males;
troublemakers came from poorer families, or from broken
homes or otherwise had out-of-school problems; and one
could identify a troublemaker by the way he or she
"looked." These assumptions will be elaborated in further
detail and tested using data gathered in the schools we
studied.

School personnel presented what can be called the
"critical mass of troublemakers" theory. Principals, for
example, talked about the number of troublemakers which a

78

school could absorb before the institution became difficult to manage. A junior high principal reported that thirty such students (in a school of 500) was about the limit and "after that all hell breaks loose." Another junior high principal, talking about the discipline problems in his school, stated, "Grade nine had thirty-five of them[3] and there wasn't anything we could do until they went on to high school. Now they're someone else's problem." Principals and teachers alike also talked about "good times" and "bad times" for their schools, based on the years when the troublemaker percentages were high or low.[4] As one teacher put it, "We had most of our troubles around 1968 at _____ [school]. There were so many troublemakers there was nothing we could do. Fire alarms went off all the time. A student sprayed the Guidance Office with a fire extinguisher." The teacher continued with an exasperated expression, "You never knew what was going to happen next; now things are better." Teachers talked about the number of troublemakers they could endure in their individual classrooms. One or two might be dealt with, but more could cause difficulties.

Related to the critical mass theory was the feeling that "good students" could be led astray by a troublemaker and that a domino-like effect was at work whenever a group of troublemakers was present in a classroom or school. Other students would inevitably be drawn into rule-breaking activities.

Principals, teachers, and students reported a series of similar assumptions about what troublemakers were like. It was agreed that the troublemaker did not like school and received low grades. Troublemakers were not seen as being active in the life of the school nor, obviously, did they have "school spirit."[5] Troublemakers were thought to be males and were always described using masculine pronouns.

Teachers saw many of the troublemakers as having special, out-of-school problems. Solving these was not related to "their job in the classroom" and was therefore the responsibility of counselors, social agency workers, or someone else, though the "someone" was not always specified. Because teachers held students themselves responsible for their misbehavior in school, teacher factors, such as the inability to hold the interest of the class, were never considered as a cause of misbehavior.[6] Teachers, in general, claimed credit for the advances made by their "good students" but accepted no responsibility for those doing less well. Parents, on the other hand, sometimes blamed the teacher for contributing to the situations which led to student misbehavior.[7] This caused occasional conflicts for principals who found themselves caught in the middle.

It was the commonly held view that troublemakers came from "poor families." This assumption fit with the view that the troublemakers often had "out-of-school problems"; many teachers assumed that students from poor families had a monopoly on such problems.[8] Teachers, in summary, saw misbehaving students as coming from poor families, as less interested in learning, as having "problems" which could not be addressed in school, and therefore as needing correction by someone outside the classroom.

Teachers also related the decline in the use of physical punishment of students to the increase in the number of troublemakers. Several teachers related the need for physical punishment to the perceived social class of the troublemakers. One stated, "The only punishment these kids from ____ [a poor neighborhood] understand is a quick slap. That's the only thing they respond to at home and it's the only thing they'd respond to here." Some teachers talked fondly of the days when physical punishment was less likely to lead to lawsuits, as discussed in the next chapter.

An Empirical Look at Troublemakers. Interviews with teachers, administrators, and students generated a number of hypotheses about troublemakers which can be tested empirically. These testable hypotheses include the assumptions that most rule violations are the product of a small percentage of students, that troublemakers come from poor homes and their families have unique characteristics, and that rule breakers are male and they do not do well academically or participate in the life of the school.

First, we will assess whether or not most school offenses are in fact committed by a small number of students. Students were asked on the questionnaires whether they had ever skipped school or cut class, and, if so, how many times they had done so "this school year." Because the surveys were administered in January, the question elicited data on the frequency of these events during the first half of the school year.[9] In addition, students in each grade from seven through twelve were asked whether they had been kicked out of a class by a teacher or suspended by a principal during the previous three years. Class cutting was the more common offense; 32.4% (N = 407) of the students in Middle City reported they had cut a class during the first half of the school year; 36.9% (N = 86) of the students in the Rural Place said they had cut a class during the same period. Skipping school for the whole day was reported less frequently--18.7% (N = 245) in Middle City and 23.5% (N = 54) in Rural Place. Each offense increased by grade level; far more seniors skipped or cut class than did seventh graders.

In Middle City 17.4% (N = 229) reported they had been kicked out of a class by January, 24.5% in Rural Place (N = 57). Being kicked out of class was not strongly related to grade level. Students in one grade level stood about as good a chance as students in any other level of being asked by a teacher to leave a class for committing an in-class offense.

In order to test the hypothesis about repeat rule-- breakers, it is necessary to focus on the total number of offenses reported by students. The following table reports the total number of rule violations or times a teacher asked each student to leave a classroom. Not all students breaking these school rules did so the same number of times. Over- all, a slight majority of those who skipped, cut, or were kicked out of a class did so only once or twice.

Table 5-1

Repetition of Rule-Breaking

	Middle City		Rural Place	
	Once or Twice	Three or More	Once or Twice	Three or More
Cutting Class	50.1%	49.9%	41.9%	58.1%
Skipping School	54.2%	45.8%	50.0%	50.0%
Being Kicked Out of Class	69.8%	30.2%	86.7%	13.3%

Those students who are the repeat offenders (three or more times), however, committed the lion's share of offenses. In Middle City 81.5% of the total class-cutting resulted from those who cut three or more times; 86.3% of the school skip- ping from students who skipped three or more times and 63.8% of the offenses which led to being sent out of a class- room were recorded by students to whom this happened three or more times. In Rural Place repeat offenders accounted for 85.6% of the cutting, 81.6% of the skipping, and 37.0% of the class removals.

Put another way, 81.5% of Middle City's class-cutting was committed by only 15.5% of its school population, 86.3% of skipping by 8.8% of the students and 63.8% of the

incidents leading to class removal by 5.2% of the students.
In Rural City 85.6% of cutting, 81.6% of skipping, and 37.0%
of the removals were committed by 21.5%, 11.6% and 2.6% of
the students, respectively. These data offer strong
empirical validation for the proposition that a small
percentage of the students in a school commit a large
percentage of the offenses.

There is also substantial overlap among the students
committing various types of offenses, as seen in Table 5-2.
Students who cut a class are three to six times more likely
to skip school or to be asked to leave a class by a teacher
than are students who report never cutting a class.

While a large percentage of students occasionally break
rules--only 30% of the students said they never had cut
class, skipped school, been kicked out of class, been to detention, or been suspended--most of the occasional violators
are not repeat rule-breakers. A small percentage, between
8 and 20%, depending on the offense, repeatedly do so.

Table 5-2

Overlap Among Offenses
Committed by Students*

		Ever Skip		Ever Kicked Out Of Class		
		Yes	No	Yes	No	
Ever Cut	Yes	50.3%	49.7%	40.8%	59.2%	(N = 741)
	No	8.2%	91.8%	15.0%	85.0%	(N = 524)

*Data drawn from all project schools.

Troublemaker Demographics. A sample of students
identified by principals as "troublemakers" were interviewed
in each school. At some point in each interview, the
student was asked to talk about his or her home life. While
some troublemakers talked about parents on welfare or about
missing fathers or mothers, many of those interviewed reported coming from middle-class homes.[10] Many students
indicated that one or both parents were employed in middle-
or upper-middle status occupations.[11]

Data from the students' questionnaires also address the
question of social class and troublemaking. Students were
asked to provide a description of their mothers' and fathers'
occupations. These were converted into numerical ratings

using the Duncan scale.[12] The numerical scores were then clustered into five groups. Higher-status occupations have higher numerical rankings. The following chart shows the distribution of fathers' Duncan scores, by percentages, in five scale clusters, for the whole student sample. The fathers' Duncan scores for those suspended are also given. About one-fourth (24.5% of the whole sample) reported fathers' occupations which placed the respondents in the lowest of the five clusters. Almost the same percentage of students who were suspended, 28.4%, had fathers whose occupations fell in the same cluster. The pattern continues across all of the clusters, with only a slight, statistically insignificant grouping of the suspended students in the lower occupational scale clusters.[13] The next table considers the same question and mothers' occupations. The working mothers of students who were suspended were somewhat more likely to have lower-status occupations.

Table 5-3

Distribution of Fathers' Occupations

| | Duncan Scale Cluster | | | | | | |
	1	2	3	4	5	Total	
Sus-pended Students	28.4%	27.0%	24.3%	16.2%	4.1%	100.0%	(N=74)
Whole Sample	24.5%	23.2%	29.0%	22.3%	11.0%	100.0%	(N=1190)

To consider other forms of troublemaking, the students in Middle City were divided into two groups using fathers' Duncan occupational score and merging occupations 1-69 into one group called "lower" and 70-99 into a group called "higher" (total N = 996).[14] As Table 5-5 illustrates, students in the lower occupational status group were slightly more likely to commit offenses and, interestingly, were more likely to be caught when they did break rules. They were also more likely to be punished for misbehavior, even when the number of offenses committed in the last year is controlled for.

Table 5-4

Distribution of Mothers' Occupations

| | Duncan Scale Cluster | | | | | | |
	1	2	3	4	5	Total	
Sus-pended Students	47.1%	9.8%	23.5%	19.6%	0.0%	100.0%	(N=51)
Whole Sample	27.9%	9.2%	29.1%	32.7%	1.1%	100.0%	(N=1190)

Part of the perception that lower-class kids cause all the trouble, then, may be due to the fact that higher-status kids avoid apprehension for rule-breaking.[15] Our observations suggest that teachers and principals do not expect kids

Table 5-5

Offenses Reported,
Apprehension, and Punishment Rates for
Students Based on Fathers' Economic Status

	Lower (1-69)	Higher (70-99)	
Ever Cut	42.7%	30.3%	*
Ever Skip	26.1%	17.1%	**
Ever Kicked Out	25.4%	21.1%	NS
Caught Cutting	35.3%	28.3%	NS
Caught Skipping	32.3%	18.2%	NS
Given Detention	37.2%	27.4%	**
Five Detentions	17.2%	3.8%	**

*Significant at .001 level
**Significant at .01 level
NS - Not Significant

from high-status homes to break rules and may be oblivious to some rule violations committed by these students when they occur. Alternatively, misbehavior of higher-status children may be excused more readily. In any case, even when the school's own offenses are used as the measure, it is clear that troublemakers cannot be fairly characterized as lower-class children.

There are, however, nonclass differences between the troublemakers and other students. The troublemakers are more likely to have a missing parent, though not in numbers which one would expect after listening to teachers and principals talk about broken homes as a cause of troublemaking. Broken homes are considered in the next table. "Perfect" students reported they never cut class, skipped school, were assigned detention, or were suspended. "In-between" students reported one or more cuts, skips, or detentions, but never were suspended.

Table 5-6

Missing Parents and Student Rule-Breaking*

		Mother Missing	Father Missing
	Perfect (N=405)	2.2%	9.2%
Students	In-Between (N=774)	2.8%	13.7%
	Suspended (N=105)	8.5%	23.8%

*Significant at .001 level

The suspended students also are somewhat less likely to have parents who finished college. Of those suspended, 17.2% reported fathers with college degrees and 10.7% reported mothers with degrees, as opposed to 33.7% of the perfect students reporting fathers with degrees and 25.5% representing mothers with degrees.

Those who got in trouble in school were disproportionately male. This is seen in the following table.

While most ascribed status characteristics proved to be unrelated or only weakly related to troublemaking, in-school attainment proved closely related. Those who did well in school were far less likely to get in trouble.[16] This was true for every type of rule infraction and is dramatically illustrated in Table 5-8 which compares suspended students

Table 5-7

Sex of Student and School Behavior*

		Male	Female
	Perfect (N=408)	45.6%	54.4%
Students	In-Between (N=782)	52.7%	47.3%
	Suspended (N-105)	63.8%	36.2%

*Significant at .001 level

with the other two groups and considers grades received by the students. Post-high-school objectives expressed by the students in the three groups also differed. The "perfect" students saw themselves attending college after high school, while the troublemaker students predicted that they would be entering the work force or were uncertain about what the future might hold. In the perfect group 61.4% planned to attend college and 12.5% felt they would go to work after high school. Among the troublemakers 18.9% thought they would attend college and 42.1% saw a job after high school. The closer the troublemakers got to grade 12, the less likely they were to say they were college bound.

Table 5-8

Grades Received and School Behavior*

	A's & B's	C's and D's
Perfect (N=405)	62.2%	37.8%
In-Between (N=782)	44.2%	55.8%
Suspended (N-103)	18.4%	81.6%

*Significant at .001 level

Overall, the troublemakers were less involved in the school than those who never broke rules. They received lower grades, and few had expectations of attending college after high school. As predicted by teachers and principals, the troublemakers were also more likely to be male and to have a parent missing. Over 70%, however, had both parents present in the home, and parents' occupations were generally unrelated to troublemaking. Major assumptions made by school personnel, then, were not sustained empirically. The consequences of these misperceptions will be discussed below.

There were other differences between the troublemakers and those who didn't break rules. Troublemakers reported more unfairness throughout the discipline system than did students who were never in trouble. Clearly, the trouble-makers had more first-hand experience with that system, though all students in school see discipline at work on a regular basis. But while unfairness was perceived by a sizable percentage of all students, personal familiarity was more often associated with the feeling that the system was not operating fairly. This can be seen on the general fairness question, which asked the respondent to check whether teachers (or students or principals) were fair all the time, most of the time, sometimes, seldom, or never. All or most-of-the-time percentages are reported in Table 5-9. On all three questions the students who are the troublemakers see less fairness in the school environment. Specific items were also included which asked students to indicate who received preferential treatment in the school disciplinary system. Again, while many students saw some discrimination, it was felt most intensely by those frequently in contact with the system. (Preferential treatment is discused in more detail in Chapter 6.)

Table 5-9

Student Perceptions of Fairness and School Behavior*

		Fairness of . . .**		
		Teachers	Principals	Other Students***
	Perfect	75.4%	74.3%	44.9%
Students	In-Between	67.3%	60.5%	40.2%
	Suspended	50.4%	46.6%	35.7%

*Significant at the .001 level

**Fairness all or most of the time.
***Did students treat teacher fairly.

Table 5-10

Preferential Treatment of Students*

	Worse for Inactive Students	Worse for Poor Students	Worse for Older Students	Better for Team Players
Perfect	26.7%	7.4%	6.0%	39.1%
In-Between	39.9%	13.1%	8.6%	54.1%
Suspended	56.3%	16.7%	19.4%	56.3%

*Significant at .001 level

It is also interesting to look at the effect of frequent contact with the discipline system and the subsequent deterrent effect of that system. Students were asked about the punishment they perceived as flowing from apprehension for a variety of offenses which were listed; the student could check "a lot of trouble," "some trouble," or "no trouble." There are some students who feel they will not get in a "lot of trouble" for committing even the most serious in-school offenses, though it is uncertain whether this is due in part to optimism about the chances for escaping detection, braggadocio on the part of respondents, or perceptions regarding juvenile justice penalties generally. In any event, the troublemaker group consistently reported that they would get in less trouble for committing major infractions than did those who never broke a rule. Experience with the system, then, is associated with decreasing fear of system sanctions.

On the other hand, when minor infractions like wandering in the halls or in-class talking are considered, more of the troublemakers felt they would get in a lot of trouble for these violations than did the perfect students. While the percentages are not large, responses to this item suggest support for a claim advanced by some troublemakers that their every move is open to scrutiny and that they are punished for some violations which, if they were committed by a different student, would not result in punishment at all.

The Troublemaker Profile. From all these data a picture of the troublemaker begins to emerge. While family characteristics are not strongly associated with trouble-making, as school personnel suggest, in-school behavior and

Table 5-11

Student Perceptions of Punishment*

Minor Infractions**

	Talking	Wandering	Swearing at Student
Perfect	1.0%	5.2%	3.5%
In-Between	3.0%	5.1%	4.5%
Suspended	8.5%	9.4%	8.6%

Major Infractions**

Liquor	Committing Crime	Possessing Weapon	Using or Drugs
Perfect	85.0%	74.8%	82.8%
In-Between	80.0%	64.5%	74.8%
Suspended	72.1%	58.7%	66.3%

	Assaulting Teacher	Setting False Alarm	Fighting
Perfect	86.2%	87.8%	52.8%
In-Between	79.4%	85.1%	39.0%
Suspended	69.5%	72.4%	38.1%

*Students reporting they would get in a "lot of trouble" for the offense. **Significant at the .001 level.

reported future plans are significant. Especially when interview data are considered (see the appendix following this chapter), it can be argued that the troublemakers see much less relevance between what they are expected to do in school and what they plan to accomplish after school. They often reported in interviews that their courses were "dumb," that teachers' expectations were unrealistic, and that they failed to see how their courses would be useful in the future. While these arguments are clearly not novel, they further delineate the link between student disenchantment and school misbehavior.[17]

The data also suggest that assumptions about troublemakers held by teachers and administrators are not accurate. The troublemakers do not disproportionately have the social class backgrounds which school personnel assume they have. Likewise they do not have the overwhelming home problems attributed to them. And, when interviewed, the troublemakers themselves place substantial weight on in-school factors as a source of their misbehavior. Teachers, however, focus on inaccurate or exaggerated out-of-school sources.

Most troublemakers derive a part of their in-school identities from causing trouble, and some maximize their satisfaction by thinking of creative ways to cause trouble. The troublemakers enjoy their reputations as rule-breakers and, in fact, were quite well known by other students. Some play "cops and robbers" games with administrators and, while they probably wouldn't admit it, the administrators derived some satisfaction from the game as well. Principals, for example, boasted to their teachers when they had "solved" a tough case, and it was clear that principals saw that they would be judged by teachers both by the way they handled cases sent to the office and by the extent to which they controlled in-school trouble.

The interviews also suggest that troublemakers were unhappy being in class and often caused trouble simply to get out of a class they didn't like. This finding was further supported by the fact that most of the troublemakers reported that there were classes which they liked and in which they caused no trouble. Most of the troublemakers had little use for most of what went on in school; they did poorly and seem frustrated because other students were receiving in-class support from teachers while they received no encouragement. And they saw no connection between classwork and what they wanted to do after school, if, in fact, they had such aspirations. Some of the troublemakers appeared to have little to look forward to at all.

The troublemakers also did not worry about penalties. As one student put it, "I'm never going to be a doctor or anything, so getting hauled out of class won't hurt me." Others welcomed the chance to get out of class. For the troublemakers, suspension was the best way of all to avoid being in school.

Troublemakers are a distinct group within the structure of the school, but the commonly held notions about what they are like do not seem to be particularly accurate. Most troublemakers are not from the lower class, nor are they suffering from severe character disorders. They are, instead, students who don't like being in school and don't like most of their classes. Some are waiting for a chance to leave. In the meantime, they obtain satisfaction by breaking school rules.

B. Troubled Schools

Administrators of larger systems can identify schools in which discipline problems occur more frequently. These we characterize as "troubled schools." Junior High School X in Middle City was known as such a school. Teachers in School

Table 5-12

Teacher Reports of Discipline Problems --
Three Junior High Schools

Teacher reports of:	School X	School Y	School Z
A prank or practical joke	57.6%	46.2%	32.5%
Vandalism to teacher's property	66.7%	30.8%	25.0%
Verbal abuse (threats, swearing)	92.6%	64.2%	70.8%
Physical attack	22.2%	3.8%	0.0%
Problems leading to suspension	74.1%	32.0%	54.2%
Other acts by students (thefts, extortion)	29.7%	26.9%	8.3%
	(N = 27)	(N = 26)	(N = 24)

X constantly reported they were on the "front lines" while their colleagues in other junior highs had "an easy time." As with their characterizations of the troublemakers, teachers in School X did not have a full understanding of their own school and the extent to which it did and did not differ from the others. This section will use both interview and aggregate data to discover how School X differed from the other two junior high schools in the community.

Based on teachers' experience with discipline problems, School X had more reported misbehavior than the other two junior high schools.[18] While the differences were not large on some items, teachers at X did report more problems in

every category than did the teachers at the other two
schools. When asked about the problems they observed,
then, teachers at School X saw more problems in their school
than did teachers at the other two junior high schools. The

Table 5-13

Observed Misbehavior By Teachers and Students --
Three Junior High Schools

Misbehavior Observed Frequently:	School X	School Y	School Z
Students Fighting With Other Students			
Teacher Observation	37.0%	4.2%	4.2%
Student Observation	13.8%	8.7%	7.8%
Stealing			
Teacher Observation	14.8%	0.0%	0.0%
Student Observation	11.6%	10.6%	3.7%
Students Using Liquor or Drugs			
Teacher Observation	14.8%	0.0%	4.2%
Student Observation	12.6%	12.6%	11.5%
Talking Back to a Teacher			
Teacher Observation	77.8%	34.6%	13.0%
Student Observation	52.2%	39.3%	36.0%
Swearing at a Teacher			
Teacher Observation	29.6%	4.0%	4.2%
Student Observation	10.5%	7.3%	7.8%

students in X, however, didn't agree with this assessment.
(Percentages seeing such misbehavior "frequently" are
reported.[19]) Students saw approximately the same level of
misbehavior in all three schools.

There was also more unfairness reported at School X by
students, though the differences were not large, as seen in
Table 5-14. While School X is at the margin on most of
these items, the magnitude of the differences did not

correspond to the interview and observational data which led
us to expect greater divergence.

Table 5-14

Fairness "All" or "Most" of the Time --
Three Junior High Schools

	School X	School Y	School Z
Teachers Treat Students Fairly	49.3%	65.2%	65.8%
Administrators Treat Students Fairly	58.5%	43.9%	67.3%
Students Treat Teachers Fairly	24.7%	38.6%	42.0%

We expected to find empirical evidence that X was the
scene of substantial misbehavior on the part of students,
since teachers in School X consistently reported that they
were teaching in the school with the most problems. They
felt besieged by discipline problems and reacted by staying
in their classrooms, refraining from standing in halls as
classes changed, and never going near student restrooms.
This created the feeling, both real and imagined, that the
halls were open zones for student misbehavior.

School X teachers pictured themselves as besieged,
without allies, unsupported by administrators and parents,
and facing an unruly crowd of students whom they
characterized using unflattering terms. Some teachers called
the students "animals." Every disciplinary incident was
used as further evidence that the school was on the verge of
collapse, and many teachers indicated that they were seeking
transfers to other schools in the system.

The teachers were also feuding with their principal.
The principal had placed letters of reprimand in the files of
several teachers for using too much physical force in handling altercations with students. These letters were the
subject of a union grievance filed by the teachers in
question. Teachers also said they were not "supported"
when they sent students to the office. One teacher's
comments represented both points of view. "We send kids
down. Nothing happens. The kids get a free day or two
off, or maybe get a lecture, and they come back and start
up right where they leave off. The Office could do a lot
more to back up teachers. The principal should pressure

downtown [the central system administration] to get more
effective rules and disciplinary procedures. I think the
administration is going down the wrong track on a number of
things." Teachers in School X responded to the question,
"What type of behavior by administrators do you think contributes to student discipline problems?" by stressing that
their principal was not strict enough and allowed too many
second chances, was not sufficiently involved, and didn't
back up teachers. (See Table 5-15.) In fact, the principal
at X was more likely to use suspension or other formal penalties than were the teachers at the other junior highs.

Teachers in School X also felt that the district's Student Code made students more outspoken and harder to
discipline. They reported that the Code contributed to many
of their problems, through the Code itself was hardly
referred to at all in the day-to-day life of the school. In
fact, in School Z where the Code actually was used to form
the basis of the disciplinary regime--it was referred to by
the principal when students were disciplined--the Code was

Table 5-15

Teachers Responding
Administrators Not Strict Enough

	N	Percent
School X	19	82.6
School Y	8	38.1
School Z	4	23.5

widely supported by teachers. This suggested to us that
the teachers in School X were using every possible argument
to present a picture of themselves as helpless to handle
discipline problems and as governed by incompetents. While
School X did have a slightly higher level of reported discipline problems, the rhetoric used to describe the situation
was greatly exaggerated.

Social Class and the Troubled School. Part of the
teachers' portrait of School X was based on the frequently
asserted claim that they were teaching "all the poor kids."
They combined this view with the assumption that such
children were not really interested in education and that
they caused a disproportionate amount of trouble.[20] This
latter assumption is the same characterization of

troublemakers which was examined in the previous section, expanded to include the composition of the whole school.

Because the perceived social class difference between the students in X and the other two schools had such important behavioral consequences, it needs to be looked at closely. A survey question instructed teachers to pick the social class which they thought best represented their student body. The responses to that question are contained in the following table.

Table 5-16

Perceived Social Class of
Students in Three Junior High Schools

	Working Class	Lower Middle	Middle	Upper Middle	
School X	43.8%	46.9%	9.4%	0.0%	(N = 32)
School Y	6.5%	22.6%	51.6%	19.4%	(N = 31)
School Z	10.3%	13.8%	58.6%	17.2%	(N = 29)

Duncan occupational scores were combined to form five clusters for the parents of students in each of the three schools. These showed an occupational distribution as shown in Table 5-17. While School X did have a higher percentage of students whose fathers had lower-status occupations, the percentages were not as large as one would have anticipated on the basis of the teachers' perceptions. In reality, each school had its share of students from lower socioeconomic groups. Each also had between 100 and 200 students participating in federally supported lunch programs, another indication of the distribution of students from low-income families.

Students from lower-income families, about a third of the enrollment, tended to be invisible to teachers in schools with a more middle-class population, while the presence of a bare majority of children from working-class homes caused the middle-class children in X to disappear in the eyes of the teachers. The class composition was extremely important to the teachers' perception of the school in general because of their strong characterization of middle-class children as those most interested in learning and of lower-class students as troublemakers.[21]

Table 5-17

Fathers' Duncan Occupational
Scores -- Three Junior High Schools

		Duncan Scale Cluster				
	1	2	3	4	5	
School X	26.0%	30.0%	28.7%	13.3%	2.0%	(N=150)
School Y	21.8%	16.5%	15.3%	32.9%	13.5%	(N=170)
School Z	13.0%	19.5%	13.0%	29.2%	25.3%	(N=154)

School X, then, was viewed as doubly cursed by teachers. It did have a few more discipline problems and a higher percentage of working-class children. The two factors, however, were interpreted by the teachers at X in ways far more extreme than appears warranted by the data.[22] The problems were magnified and a self-perpetuating cycle of name-calling and guilt-assignment followed. At School X, no one liked anyone else very much. Teachers, students, and administrators called one another names and engaged in extreme stereotyping. Students were quick to detect that there was much staff unhappiness and that expectations for improvement were lacking.[23] There was no "school spirit" and few of the participants looked forward to the start of the school day.[24] School X was not that different, but those in the school though it was, and this had a substantial impact on behavior. Everyone in the school behaved as if it were substantially unlike the other schools in the community.

C. Teachers and Troublemaking

Some teachers frequently observed students breaking rules while others reported they never saw students violating them. For example, 20.5% of the 190 teachers "frequently" saw students vandalizing school property while 15.8% "never" observed the same incidents. Some teachers, then, seem to miss rule-breaking which other teachers find commonplace. As a consequence, some teachers reported they were far more often involved in school disciplinary incidents which led to the suspension of a student; those who saw more frequent rule violations were much more often involved in suspension of students. Of the 207 teachers we studied, 45.9% had been involved in a suspension of a student in the last three years. Most of these, 73.5%, were involved in a small number of cases, from 1 to 5. A few teachers, 8 of the 207, were involved in 11 or more suspensions in the last three years.

The search for variables related to frequent observation of discipline problems or to involvement in suspension cases proved unrewarding. It might be suspected, for example, that new teachers would see more rule-breaking than would veteran teachers who had been in the schools for many years. But this did not prove to be the case. There were some new teachers who saw lots of rule-breaking and some who saw none at all, even within the same schools. Likewise, age, sex, teacher's family background, participation in extracurricular events, and a large number of personal variables, were unrelated to observed incidents. It is possible, of course, that some teachers are oblivious to rule-breaking, that they ignore such offenses and somehow don't see them, or that students misbehave only in the presence of certain teachers and are careful to avoid rule-breaking in the presence of others.

Teachers who see more rule-breaking have different attitudes about the use of disciplinary punishments than do the other teachers. They are more likely to favor greater use of serious sanctions, such as suspension or expulsion, to deal with students breaking the rules. The teachers who see more disorder also favor a more controlled student environment. Wanting more exclusionary discipline was also related to favoring a "closed school" (all students in assigned areas at all times). Of those favoring more exclusion, 55.6% preferred the closed school, compared to 30.5% support for closed campus among those who wanted the same or fewer exclusions.

Teacher Definitions of Appropriate Conduct. Some of the differences among teachers' observations of rule-breaking can be explained by variance in the personal definitions of acceptable student behavior. One teacher's verbal abuse, for example, might be another's view of a "typical, active student." Thus teachers may not see the same things, though several might witness the same event. One teacher might view the use of a four-letter word as insubordination or a threat to authority requiring action by the principal, while another might see it as something best handled quietly in class. Some teachers, in other words, are authoritarian and inflexible while others are more relaxed and less rigid. Pupil control exercised by teachers has been related to a variety of teacher personality variables.[25]

Again, most personal teacher variables are not related to the preference to handle matters personally, as opposed to using formal sanctions. The subject taught by the teacher, however, was related to the teacher's preference for more or less order in the classroom and to the way the teacher would respond to student misbehavior or autonomy. This is seen in Table 5-18, where teachers are grouped by subject taught and the classroom structure preferred. The findings in this table correspond to the literature which suggests that math and science teachers are less open to autonomy in classes and more favorably disposed toward a lecture format with more order.[26] In addition to classroom structure, the math-science teachers also reported that they felt significantly more hampered by court decisions; 79.7% of the math-science teachers expressed this sentiment compared to 49.7% of the English-social studies teachers.

Table 5-18

Classroom Preferred and Subject Taught*

		Classroom Preferred		
	Open	Somewhat Structured	Very Structured	
Math-Sciences	1.8%	45.6%	52.6%	(N=57)
English-Social Studies	4.8%	66.7%	28.6%	(N=63)

*Significant at the .01 level

In addition to having different attitudes, the math-science teachers responded to discipline problems in significantly different ways. As seen in Table 5-19, English and social studies teachers are much more likely to handle a cursing student with an in-class solution, such as a personal conversation with the offender. The math-science teachers tend to respond more with out-of-class answers. As a consequence of sending more students to the principal, more math-science teachers report involvement with school suspension than do the English-social studies teachers, as seen in Table 5-20. The math-science teachers also favored greater

Table 5-19

How Teachers Respond
to Students Who Swear at Them*

	Talk to Student Handle in Class	Send to Principal	Other Out-of-Class Solutions
Math-Science (N=59)	34.5%	39.7%	25.8%
English-Social Studies (N=67)	67.9%	27.1%	5.0%

*Significant at the .001 level

use of exclusionary discipline on the attitude survey, strongly suggesting that there is a link between teacher attitude about punishment and the subsequent administration of that punishment, even though it is principals who are the agents carrying out the penalty. Much of this relationship appears related to the discretion exercised by the teacher in sending the student to the office in the first place. In addition, the principals whom we observed considered, in varying degrees, the potential reaction of the teacher who referred the student when considering what penalty to apply. Thus it is also possible that teachers who outspokenly sought to have students suspended may have had their wish granted, particularly in marginal cases.

Table 5-20

Teacher Involvement with Out-of-School
Suspensions and Subject Taught*

	Been Involved in Suspending Students		
	Yes	No	
Math-Sciences	62.7%	37.3%	(N=59)
English-Social Studies	29.9%	70.1%	(N=67)

*Significant at the .001 level

Personal Experience With Vandalism. There is some evidence that teachers who are frequently involved in incidents in which students are sent to the office or who favor more suspensions and expulsions also experience greater personal involvement with vandalism. Of those who want greater use of both types of exclusionary discipline (N=27), for example, 66.7% reported that they had been a victim of vandalism in the last three years, compared with 27.9% among the 178 teachers who did not favor greater use of exclusion. Again, it is possible that teachers may define vandalism in different ways.

These reports of vandalism also may have their origin in the fact that such vandalism is not entirely random, but is sometimes directed at particular teachers. Several students described the ways in which they "got even" with teachers or administrators whom they felt had either been unduly severe or insulted or injured them in some way. One student talked about a hardliner and said he would like to "punch Mr. S____ " or "throw a brick through his car window." While most of these threats were undoubtedly idle boasts, several may have reflected actual student activity.[27] Teachers who reported they were more flexible in the classroom also reported they were less frequently the target of vandalism. "Being tough," then, may have unmeasured effects elsewhere within the school or in seemingly unrelated incidents which occur in school parking lots or out of school altogether.

Summary: Teachers and Trouble. While the literature on school discipline tends to group all teachers together, our research found several distinct groups of teachers, each with different perceptions and attitudes about discipline, and the amount of order needed in schools. Each group reported varying contact with students who cause trouble. A small number of teachers were uncovered who had no trouble at all in their classrooms and another small group was located which provided administrators with the bulk of their out-of-class referrals.[28]

There were also readily identified teachers in each school who, more so than their colleagues, called for more order, and a stricter enforcement of the rules.[29] These teachers tended to see more discipline problems and to experience more problems personally. Part of these differences were explained by looking at the definitions of acceptable conduct employed by these teachers. Some had much more fixed ideas about proper student conduct and granted less latitude to students when it came to speech and other forms of behavior. For example, they saw more verbal abuse because they defined more words as abusive. For a school whose staff seek a different level of order, the first step is deciding exactly how much order is needed. Reaching agreement on this will clearly not be easy. Care will have to be taken so that agreement is reached on exactly which behavior is defined as unacceptable.

Personal definitions of misbehavior, however, did not explain all of the differences observed. Some "objective" offenses, like gambling and setting false alarms, were frequently seen by some teachers and never seen by others. Some teachers, then, either exercised such selective perception as never to see rule-breaking or were never in the place where such rule-breaking occurred. A plausible interpretation of these data suggests that some teachers do not wish to be involved in disciplinary incidents. This fits with our evidence presented elsewhere that some teachers strongly held that discipline was "someone else's job," or that they were responsible for their classroom and not beyond.

Selective perceptions and different definitions of acceptable student behavior both contribute to substantial unevenness in the way student rule-breakers are treated. There are times when what happens to the student in a given situation is wholly dependent on which teacher rounds the corner to observe the student misbehavior. Suspension from school, a friendly conversation, or nothing at all are all possible outcomes of most acts of school misbehavior, depending on which teacher observes the act, and, as will be seen in the next chapter, on which student is the actor.

Appendix
A Close-Up Look:
Conversations with Troublemakers

Donna K_____ was a ninth-grade student who had been suspended from school on several occasions, once for smoking, once for repeated class disruption, and once for punching another girl in English class.[30] She described the fight as follows: "This one girl had been looking down her nose at me. She was a real teacher's pet. So I fixed her--I punched her out. Now she doesn't bother me so much anymore." Donna reported that she was angry about "teacher's pets" in general. "Kids who dress poorly get picked on more. Teacher's pets and those fancy-looking girls get whatever they want and never get yelled at when they talk or make jokes. But that's just the way everything is. Some people get treated better than the rest. We just have to take care of ourselves."

Donna admitted breaking many school rules, though she never got in any trouble in two of her classes. "I like art and science sometimes. I don't make any trouble there." Later in the interview she explained, "In most classes they never seem to teach us any good stuff. Art is fun because you can make things. Science is good every once in a while." In some of her other classes Donna caused trouble just to be kicked out of a class she didn't like. "Mrs. M. [a teacher] tries to keep me after school a lot. Once in a while, though, she sends me down to the office. I love getting out of that class, even though I end up in trouble."

Donna was well known as a defiant troublemaker, except by her art and science teachers, and she was the subject of occasional discussions in the teacher's lounge. The teachers would swap "Donna stories" and wonder how long it would be until she decided to drop out of school or until she was incarcerated by the juvenile authorities. Donna's parents were considered "noncooperative" by school officials, and occasionally they called the principal to complain that teachers were picking on their daughter. Wherever she went, Donna seemed to leave a wake of troublemaking incidents, and her teachers were looking forward to her graduation from junior high school. One teacher told the interviewer, however, "We won't be out of the woods then, though. Donna's got a younger sister whom I've heard is even worse."

Gary was also a ninth grader, described by the interviewer as short, overweight, and poorly dressed. He reported that other kids teased him about his size, lack of physical dexterity, and the fact that he lives in a house trailer. When this teasing occurred, generally in math class, both Gary and his opponent often were sent to the office. When asked to explain what happened then, Gary said, "It's like my math book. The problems are a little different, but the outcome is always the same. I get yelled at, kicked out of class, and then sent down to the office. They send me back to class sometimes and sometimes I just go to the IMC and do my math problems."

A project observer was in the office on one of the days that Gary was sent out of math class. He reported that the office secretary, who was quite friendly with Gary, gave him a warm welcome and urged him to get some work done while waiting for the class period to end. He was a repeat visitor to the office and each time the script seemed to be the same. Sometimes the secretary just let Gary run errands for her. As she explained, "He isn't a bad kid at all. Other kids pick on him and know they can hurt his feelings or get him mad. It isn't fair."

Gary reported that it is hard being known as a kid who causes trouble. "Some teachers pick out kids to get. Most of the time the kids are the real bad ones who get in trouble a lot, but not always. Yesterday Mr. A____ shoved me up against a locker for being late to class. I told him I'd been in the office doing work for Mrs. M____ [the school secretary] but he didn't believe me. He just called me a 'fat little bastard,' shoved me up against the locker outside of the classroom, and told me to go to the office. Mr. B____ [the assistant principal] knew I'd been helping Mrs. M____, but there wasn't anything he could do about it. He won't take the side of a student against a teacher, so that was it."

Gary confirmed what Donna and most of the other troublemakers told the project staff--there were some teachers that never had any trouble in their classrooms. As Gary described it, "Mr. L____ just talks serious-like at the beginning of his class and that shuts the whole class up for an hour. Nothing serious ever happens there." The same was not true in Mr. C____'s class. "Sometimes you can watch Mr. C____ get angry. When that happens, the kids act bad until he sends a whole bunch of them down to the office."

Gary also represented another commonly held troublemaker attitude--he and most troublemakers thought that schools needed rules. Troublemakers were not anarchists; in fact, they were often more order-oriented than the "perfect" students. Gary didn't think that the rules were wisely enforced. When asked what he would do about discipline if he were the principal, he responded, "I think I would keep most of the rules we have. Schools should have discipline. You have to make it so kids don't pick on each

other. It is also good to have classes that run pretty good.
We can't learn much if kids are fooling around too much."
Gary also said he would do away with "silly rules" like
having to wear white socks in gym class. He talked about
how hard it was to get rules changed and how he and several of his classmates were forced to run laps in gym when
they showed up wearing colored socks. "We kept at it," he
reported proudly, "and now it doesn't matter what color
socks you wear."

There are times when Gary likes being sent to the
office. As he put it, "I feel like somebody wants to help me
out," when he receives a sympathetic ear for his problems.
Many of the troublemakers enjoyed the attention that getting
into trouble brought them.

Dick H_____ was another troublemaker who liked the
attention that breaking school rules brought him. Dick was
interviewed in the school's detention room where students
spent fifty minutes after the close of the school day
carefully supervised by the detention teacher. Dick had
established an ongoing relationship with Mr. J_____, the
detention supervisor. Mr. J_____ would joke with Dick, and
the two would work together on Dick's school work. As
Dick later explained, "Mr. J_____ is really nice, not phony
like the rest of my teachers." This interview suggested that
one of the rewards of being a troublemaker may be close
contact with a helpful teacher.

Dick could no longer explain the specific offense for
which he had been assigned detention, since he committed so
many. He was, in effect, serving an indeterminate sentence. Dick was much smaller than the rest of his classmates and seemed to compensate for his size by being
unusually aggressive. He had, the day before, punched a
much larger student in the mouth, though he now admitted
he had made a mistake. "I thought he was going to hit me,
so I hit him first. But I was wrong. He really was going
to close his locker." For hitting the student he had been
given two weeks in detention. Several other weeks had been
assigned for having a cigarette in his pocket when the
principal searched him one day and several more because he
was always late for school. He had been suspended from
school for that as well. Now he was picked up in the
morning by the detention hall teacher, so his tardiness had
ended.

Dick reported that he, like the other troublemakers
interviewed, had some classes in which he never caused
trouble and others in which he did. As he put it, "No one
causes trouble in Mrs. J_____'s class. She's so strict no one
would live if they acted bad." In general, though, most of
Dick's problems were related to offenses which occurred in

the halls and lunchroom. He described how he and other students had started a fight with mashed potatoes one noon when the lights went out. "That got me four weeks."

Dick and many other regulars in the detention hall really didn't mind spending time there. In fact, they appeared to derive a substantial portion of their in-school identity from being troublemakers. They talked manfully about "the time they had to do," and in general seemed to enjoy the camaraderie of the detention hall. They compared notes about their offenses and enjoyed boasting about them. And, when they had the chance, as in the mashed potato incident, they enjoyed plotting creative ways to make trouble since, as Dick confided, "the lights didn't go out by accident."[31]

Just as Dick and other troublemakers enjoyed playing cat and mouse with the school authorities, so too did the principals and assistant principals enjoy matching their wits against troublemakers. At least one whodunnit was acted out in each of the schools where project observers were stationed. In one instance, an obscene note had been pushed through the ventilation slot in a cheerleader's locker, and the assistant principal set out, by comparing handwriting samples obtained from student English themes, to discover which of several "usual suspects" had committed the offense. While the detective work failed--the principal guessed wrong, even after obtaining the advice of several teachers familiar with the students' handwriting--the person who wrote the note was eventually collared. In this case the principal brought in students from the likely group and, keeping them separate, told each one in order, "I know it was Cathy" or "I know it was Anne who wrote the note" until one of the perpetrator's friends finally admitted that the vice-principal had guessed correctly. Seeing how much the administrators enjoyed these activities forced one interviewer to conclude that if schools didn't have enough discipline problems some would have to be invented to keep administrators happy.

NOTES

[1]For a look at the effects of stratifying students into groups, in both formal and informal ways, see Aage Bottger Sørensen, "Organizational Differentiation of Students and Education Opportunity," 43 Sociology of Education 355 (Fall, 1970).

[2]There is a large literature on the labeling of deviant behavior. The "labeling theory" suggests that once a

person is labeled as deviant further misbehavior results as a consequence of the label, in part because it is expected from the deviant and in part because the deviant comes to accept the label. See, for example, Shlomo Shoham, The Mark of Cain: The Stigma Theory of Crime and Social Deviation (Dobbs Ferry, N.Y.: Oceana Publications, Inc., 1970); Edwin M. Schur, Labeling Deviant Behavior (New York: Harper and Row, Publishers, 1971); Erving Goffman, Stigma (Englewood Cliffs: Prentice-Hall, Inc., 1963).

[3]Emphasis was the respondent's.

[4]On the creation of shared myths by teachers regarding the school in which they work, see Seymour B. Sarason, The Culture of the School and the Problem of Change (Boston: Allyn and Bacon, 1973).

[5]For a thoughtful look at the labelling of behavior problems by teachers, see Fritz Redl, "Disruptive Behavior in the Classroom," 80 School Review 569 (August, 1975).

[6]See Frederic J. Medway, "Causal Attributions for School-Related Problems: Teacher Perceptions and Teacher Feedback," 71 Journal of Educational Psychology 6 (1979).

[7]Joseph Guttmann, "Pupils', Teachers' and Parents' Causal Attributions for Problem Behavior at School," 76 Journal of Educational Research 1 (1982).

[8]See W. Gordon West, "Adolescent Deviance and the School," 6 Interchange 2, 49 (1975) for a discussion of the presumption that in-school and out-of-school problems are linked.

[9]See Chapter 1 for full information on the project.

[10]For a discussion of the lengthy list of home variables which might be related to school discipline problems and an indication of previous research on these factors, see Robert Friedman, "School Behavior Disorders and the Family," in Robert Friedman, ed., Family Roots of School Learning and Behavior Disorders (Springfield, Ill: Charles C. Thomas, Publishers, 1973).

[11]Earlier research indicated that teachers have markedly different perceptions of their jobs when they were teaching lower-class children. Teachers working with lower-class children see their jobs as more "custodial." See R. O. Carlson, "Environmental Constraints and Organizational

Consequences: The Public School and Its Clients," in D. E. Griffiths, ed., Behavioral Science and Educational Administration (Chicago: University of Chicago Press, 1964). For another perspective on how teachers respond to poor children, see Lorraine Hayes Braun, Donald J. Willower, and Patrick D. Lynch, "School Socioeconomic Status and Teacher Pupil Control Behavior," 9 Urban Education 3 (October, 1974). This line of research owes much to August B. Hollingshead, Elmtown's Youth (New York: John Wiley, 1949).

[12]The questions read, "Is your father [mother] presently employed? If so, what does he [she] do? Please name specific job, such as carpenter, doctor, etc." These were then coded on the basis of the Duncan occupational scale. Responses were divided into five clusters, each representing twenty points on the one hundred point scale. See Otis Dudley Duncan, "A Socioeconomic Index for All Occupations," in Albert Reiss, Jr., ed., Occupation and Social Status (New York: Free Press, 1961).

[13]Looking at the issue another way, students who never get in trouble report higher-status fathers' occupations in slightly higher numbers:

	Duncan Scale Clusters					
	1	2	3	4	5	Total
Perfect Students (N=326)	15.0%	23.0%	19.9%	23.9%	18.1%	100.0%
Whole Sample (N=1190)	24.5%	23.2%	19.0%	22.3%	11.0%	100.0%

"Perfect" students are those reporting they never cut a class, were asked to leave a class, skipped school, were assigned detention, or were suspended from school.

[14]"Lower" includes such occupations as factory worker, and truck driver. "Higher" includes white-collar management and professional occupations.

[15]On the powerful weight of teacher expectations in shaping and determining actual behavior see Aaron V. Cicourel and John I. Kitsuse, The Educational Decision-Makers (Indianapolis: Bobbs-Merrill Company, Inc., 1963), especially Chapter I; and James E. Rosenbaum, Making Inequality (New York: John Wiley and Sons, Inc., 1976) which looks at the question while focusing on high school tracking systems.

[16]This finding is supported by earlier research using elementary school data which found that students who get into trouble in school had significantly different intelligence, scholastic achievement, scholastic abilities, vocational aptitude, and personality characteristics when compared with students who didn't get into trouble. See Daniel L. Duke, "Who Misbehaves? A High School Studies Its Discipline Problems," 12 Educational Administration Quarterly 3 (Fall, 1976).

[17]This connection was first charted by Arthur L. Stinchcombe in Rebellion in a High School (New York: Quadrangle Books, 1964). He wrote, "The student who grasps clear connection between current activity and future status tends to regard school authority as legitimate, and to obey. The problem of order, then, is created by the inability of the school to realistically offer any desirable status beyond high school to some of its students" (p. 9).

[18]The questions read, "In the last three years, have you been the victim of. . .."

[19]Both teachers and students were asked, "How often have you seen students doing these things in your school?" Respondents were given the option of checking frequently, sometimes, rarely, or not at all.

[20]On the class differences between teachers and students, both perceived and real, and the effect this has on discipline, see David H. Hargreaves, Social Relations in a Secondary School (London: Routledge and Kegan Paul, 1967), especially Chapter 5.

[21]These class differences lead directly to a discussion of the relationship among the economic structure, dominant capitalist values, and the schools. See Samuel Bowles and Herbert Gintis, Schooling in Capitalist America (New York: Basic Books, 1976).

[22]Once the labeling process is employed, it is then used to provide "help" for the students just labeled, in the form of tracking and other methods to try to "save" some of the students perceived as college-bound, and as part of the rationale for urging students and their parents to sign exemption forms after the student reaches the age of 16; these forms have the effect of removing the student from the school altogether. For a helpful discussion of the literature on labeling and language, see Michael W. Apple, "Common Sense Categories and Curriculum Thought," in James B.

MacDonald and Esther Zaret, eds., Schools in Search of Meaning (Washington: Association for Supervision and Curriculum Development, 1975).

[23] For another look at how teacher stereotypes are received and interpreted by students, see Gerry Rosenfeld, "Shut Those Thick Lips! Can't You Behave Like a Human Being?" in Joan I. Roberts and Sherie K. Akinsanya, eds., Schooling in the Cultural Context (New York: David McKay Company, Inc., 1976). Several other articles in Part III of the Roberts-Akinsanya book examine the cultural assumptions made by teachers and the effects of these assumptions on students.

[24] While much of the analysis of troublemakers and troubled schools has focused on the apparent effects of social class to explain behavior, other factors are important to consider. Carl F. Kaestle offers a caution with regard to seeing discipline in simple economic terms, though his concern was focused on historical interpretations of school discipline. He notes, "School discipline offered something to everyone in a time of rapid change: obedient children for anxious parents, malleable students for efficient schools, productive workers for the emerging capitalist economy, and acquiescent citizens for the frail republic." "Social Change, Discipline, and the Common School in Early Nineteenth-Century America," 9 Journal of Interdisciplinary History 1 (Summer, 1978), p. 16.

[25] See Glennelle Halpin, Gerald Halpin and Karen Harris, "Personality Characteristics and Self-Concept of Preservice Teachers Related to their Pupil Control Orientation," 50 Journal of Experimental Education 4 (1982).

[26] An earlier study found that fewer discipline problems occurred in open than in closed classrooms. The authors of that study concluded that the classroom settings contributed to different norms and standards in the open classroom, since behavior incidents were the same in both settings, but reported incidents greater in the closed setting. Our research suggests that the teachers themselves have different attitudes regarding discipline and self select the setting in which they teach. Thus it is not the setting but the teacher that is the key variable. See Daniel Solomon and Arthur J. Kendall, "Teachers' Perceptions of and Reactions to Misbehavior in Traditional and Open Classrooms," 67 Journal of Educational Psychology 4 (1975).

[27]John P. DeCecco and Arlene K. Richards argue that the use of force and anger with students results in a circular, self-perpetuating round of conflict. See especially chapters 5 and 6 in their book, Growing Pains: Uses of School Conflict (New York: Aberdeen Press, 1974).

[28]One way to look at the success of some teachers relates to the teacher's ability to recognize and deal with classroom conflict. For a whole variety of reasons, classroom settings appear to generate a significant amount of conflict. See Allan D. Rank, "Conflict in the Classroom," in Fred E. Jandt, ed., Conflict Resolution Through Communication (New York: Harper and Row, Publishers, 1973). "Successful teachers," then, may have discovered ways to utilize conflict creatively while the unsuccessful may exacerbate it. "Hardliners" may have less tolerance for disagreement, and so forth.

[29]While our research did uncover some substantial differences in the orientation and attitudes of teachers, many of the ways in which teachers interact with students are quite subtle and require careful, in-class observations over extensive periods of time. Many teacher responses to student behavior, for example, take the form of nonverbal signs on other indirect reactions. A good example of such research is Rachel Sharp and Anthony Green, with Jacqueline Lewis, Education and Social Control: A Study of Progressive Primary Education (London: Routledge and Kegan Paul, 1975). See also Michael W. Apple and Nancy R. King, "What Do Schools Teach?" 6 Curriculum Inquiry 4 (1977).

[30]All names and details in this section have been altered to disguise the identity of the students.

[31]Research has suggested that the attractiveness of vandalism and the challenge presented affect whether antisocial activities follow. See Vernon L. Allan and David B. Greenberger, "An Aesthetic Theory of School Vandalism," 24 Crime and Delinquency 3 (July, 1978).

Chapter 6

"GO TO THE OFFICE!":
SCHOOL SUSPENSIONS AND FORMAL PROCEDURES

A. Suspension and the United States Supreme Court

"What I know about court cases," one teacher reported,
"I picked up in the teachers' lounge. I guess they affect
male teachers more than females, because men are more likely
to be physical with students." "I learned about court cases
in Newsweek," said another. A third teacher suggested, "It
all depends on who you grab. Grab the dumb ones--they
don't know what the hell to do. Don't grab a lawyer's kid."
This chapter considers the impact of court decisions
and state statutes on the treatment of students, with a particular focus on exclusionary discipline. Impact will be considered in several ways: compliance with the decisions and
statutes, the effect of increased legalization on school disciplinary practices, and how the courts, in general, are
viewed by school personnel. It is the broader perspective
on the impact of the court decisions that is explored in
depth. As suggested by the opening quotations, only a few
teachers and administrators had specific knowledge of education decisions, though many felt strongly that they had been
negatively affected by them. The consequences of this situation for the school discipline system will be assessed.
We begin by looking at how the Supreme Court has
dealt with school discipline issues. Both the substance and
the language of the decisions suggest the Court is generally
unwilling to curb school administrator prerogatives. Before
looking at data from the project schools, we also examine the
assumptions about school discipline made by educational
commentators.
The court decisions and statutes considering school discipline have provided very limited procedural requirements
which must be followed before a student is suspended or

111

transferred for disciplinary purposes.[1] The substantive issues raised by the rules which the student might have violated are seldom at issue. Thus the question has not been, "Is suspension a reasonable penalty for smoking in a school lavatory?" but rather, "Ought the student be provided the opportunity to tell his or her side of the story before being suspended for smoking in a school lavatory?" Only in a few first amendment cases have substantive issues been reached.

In Goss v. Lopez,[2] the United States Supreme Court ruled that a student must be given an oral or written notice of the charges, the basis for the charges and, if they are denied, opportunity to tell his or her side of the story before a short suspension (one of ten days or less). In emergency situations where a student poses a threat to persons, property, or the academic process, the student need not be provided the opportunity before suspension, but can be given the hearing as soon as practicable thereafter.[3] In reaching this decision, Justice Byron White, writing for the 5-4 majority, reasoned that students have a constitutionally protected property interest in a free public education, because the state requirement that all students attend school creates an entitlement to that education which is protected by the Due Process Clause of the Fourteenth Amendment to the United States Constitution.[4]

In addition, Justice White argued that students have a liberty interest in their good name and reputation that is protected by the Constitution.[5] The Court majority decided that a record of misconduct can damage a student's reputation in the school and interfere with later opportunities for higher education and employment. Thus the Court also concluded that a student must be awarded due process safeguards before he or she is deprived of his or her liberty interest.

The Goss case has been cited on numerous occasions by those who feel that the Court has needlessly tampered with the prerogatives of administrators to manage the schools as they see fit. The Court, however, created very limited due process rights. Students were not provided the opportunity to call witnesses on their behalf, for example, nor were they given the right to have an attorney argue for them. Justice White himself described the skeletal due process right provided by the Goss case as "no less than what a fair-minded principal would impose."[6] Justice Lewis Powell, in his dissent, echoed this point when he stated, "Nor does the Court's due process 'hearing' appear to provide significantly more protection than that already available."[7] Powell also noted, "We have relied for generations upon the experience, good faith, and dedication of those who staff our public schools."[8]

Similar language was used by the Court in a 1969 first amendment case when it ruled that students could wear protest armbands, so long as[9] the peaceful operation of the school was not jeopardized. Justice Harlan noted in his dissent in that case,

> I am reluctant to believe that there is any disagreement between the majority and myself on the proposition that school officials should be accorded with widest authority in maintaining discipline and good order in their institutions.[10]

Courts at all levels have traditionally deferred to the expertise of school officials in most matters. As one Supreme Court justice put it, "[Schools] regulate the relationship between school management and the student based upon practical and ethical considerations which the courts know very little about and with which they are not equipped to deal."[11]

The Supreme Court also voiced its support for school administrators in the major corporal punishment case, Ingraham v. Wright.[12] James Ingraham was a junior high school student in Dade County, Florida, who received 20 licks with a paddle from school officials for being slow to respond to his teacher's instructions. This paddling resulted in a hematoma that required medical attention and kept Ingraham out of school for 11 days. Ingraham and another paddled student took their school's officials to court in an effort to recover individual damages and to obtain an injunction that would end the school's corporal punishment. After losing in the lower court, the students appealed to the Supreme Court for relief on the grounds that the paddling constituted "cruel and unusual punishment" prohibited by the eighth amendment. In addition, the students argued that they were denied due process prior to the paddling in violation of the fourteenth amendment, asking that Goss hearing rights be expanded to include this type of disciplinary sanction.

The Supreme Court in a 5-4 decision ruled against the students. This time Justice Powell wrote for the majority, stating, "In view of the low incidence of abuse, the openness of our schools, and the common law safeguards that already exist, the risk of error that may result in violation of a school child's substantive rights can only be regarded as minimal."[13] Justice Powell went on to note,

> Assessment of the need for, and the appropriate means of maintaining, school discipline is committed generally to the discretion of school authorities subject to state law . . . . Imposing

additional administrative safeguards as a constitutional requirement . . . would also entail a
significant intrusion into an area of primary
educational responsibility.[14]

The dominant language employed throughout these cases
suggests the deference which the Supreme Court has
afforded school administrators in disciplining students. Even
in the Goss decision, the Court gave great weight to the
interests of school administrators in deciding what process
was due in suspension cases. In fact, we argue that the
Goss decision afforded the appearance of due process without
sufficient substance to guard against the extremes of
administrative behavior which the decision has been read as
addressing. Assuming that a malevolent administrator is
arbitrarily seeking to punish a student, the few due process
safeguards mandated by Goss can easily be converted into a
hollow ritual if the administrator is determined to suspend a
student.

Goss was also made more limited by the Supreme Court
itself. On March 21, 1978, the Court announced its decision
in Carey v. Piphus.[15] The case concerned damages due elementary and high school students who sued under federal
codes claiming that they had suffered harm because they
were suspended without a Goss due process hearing. The
Supreme Court in Carey ruled that the suspended students
could not recover for injuries caused by the suspension
unless they could prove they had suffered real harm. The
Court went further, holding that the denial of the due
process hearing should result in only nominal damages (in
this case, one dollar), since no real harm had been demonstrated. Because it is almost impossible to show direct harm
from a suspension, this decision further weakened the impact
of the Goss decision.

The response to the Goss case in education publications
was negative and predicted that lower courts would expand
the decision, a prophecy which did not come to pass.
Commentators argued the Court ought not to have entered
the discipline arena at all, expressing concern that school
administrators would be bogged down in a mire of procedural
concerns.[16] Several suggested alternatives to court supervision of disciplinary proceedings; one proposed, for
example, that students and principals should have "nonformal
conversations" instead of hearings.[17] Following a similar
concern that informal methods ought to replace
adversariness, another called for the "investigatory model,"
or the use of impartial adjudicators to settle disputes.[18]

These commentators made a number of assumptions
regarding the Goss decision and its impact on schools.
First, they assumed, erroneously as will be seen, that school

personnel would hear of the decision and understand it. They also made assumptions about how Goss hearings would be conducted and assumptions that the parties would then be dealing with one another in ways which were not common before the decision. Each commentator also had notions about the world of school discipline, of which suspensions were just a part. Absent any study of suspension by examining its use in schools, commentators were free both to construct realities about the use of suspensions before Goss and to hypothesize about the decision's effects.[19]

In similar fashion, the debate over school suspensions as an appropriate or effective tool had been carried out in the years prior to Goss without empirical study to verify the propositions which were advanced. Proponents of suspension saw it as a "needed tool," focusing on the extent of school violence and vandalism.[20] While another pointed to the lack of systematic data on school violence,[21] not to mention the absence of evidence on the deterrent effect of suspensions in reducing such violence, he was sure that suspensions were beneficial:

> . . .suspension is one of the best available
> means to serve as a rehabilitative stimulus for
> the non-conforming or immature student, and,
> equally important, to serve as the force to
> create the most healthful pedagogical climate so
> that the greatest amount of learning possible can
> take place.[22]

One researcher looked at a nonrandom sample of 83 suspended students and found that only 18 had been suspended more than once. He saw this as evidence that "exclusion does effectively reduce or stop future serious infractions of rules."[23]

The most frequently stated benefit from suspensions, according to a survey of principals by the Children's Defense Fund, was that they "involved parents with the school."[24] This assumption posited the view that the parent would converse with school officials about the child's behavior, and that such a conversation could not occur in the absence of a school suspension. It has conversely been suggested that suspensions cause parents to be negatively disposed toward the school.[25]

Opponents of school suspension focused on lost school time, especially for the marginal student.[26] In addition, it is argued that suspensions tag the student as a troublemaker, since they are recorded on the student's record and are carried to every new teacher and school. Such records go beyond the school and may affect college entrance or employment.[27] As Charles A. Reich put it, "the school's jurisdiction lasts only three or four years, but its sentence

can last a lifetime."[28]   Finally, it has been suggested that
suspensions sometimes cause marginal students to drop out of
school altogether [29] and that they may be used to achieve de
facto segregation.[30]

B.   School Suspensions in the Project Schools

Use of Suspensions.   The Supreme Court decisions
dealing with discipline, the commentary about them, and the
literature on suspensions, more generally, all informed our
examination of school suspension. We looked for compliance,
in narrow terms, with the decisions and at the understanding of the decisions by school personnel.   We also
looked at some of the alternatives to school suspension,
including exemptions, and the voluntary withdrawal from
school of students between the ages of 16 and 18, and at the
use of in-school suspension, the required attendance of
students in special rooms supervised by assistant principals
or in-school suspension attendants.

We considered the question of the deterrent value of
suspension and recorded the offenses for which it was used.
We also talked with students who had been suspended and
compared them with others in their class. We looked for the
secondary impact of having been suspended in terms of
subsequent treatment in school.   We also considered
suspensions from the students' perspective to discover how
they viewed the event. This methodology tested most of the
assumptions about suspensions which were presented in the
opening section of this chapter.

Of the students in the six schools we studied, 137, or
9.0% of the total, reported they had been suspended from
school in the three years prior to our survey. Seventy-six
of these students indicated they had been suspended in the
preceding twelve months.   A large percentage of those
suspended, 99 of the 137, or 72.2%, reported that they had
been suspended from school more than one time.   Suspension
from school was also related to other subsequent in-school
rule-breaking which led to sanctions short of suspension.
An examination of discipline records maintained by the
principals in the schools we studied showed that about
two-thirds of those suspended were subsequently caught for
truancy and that they frequently committed other offenses
after having been suspended.

About 80% of those suspended from school answered the
follow-up question indicating the offense they had committed
which led to the suspension. Thirty-three percent of the
students said they were suspended for smoking, 17% for
cutting class, 10% for throwing something (usually

snowballs), 9% for use of drugs or alcohol, and 24% for assorted other offenses.[31] As observed in the Children's Defense Fund study of school suspensions,[32] most of the suspensions were for nonviolent offenses. In addition, almost all were for violations of rules which prohibited conduct not similarly restricted outside the school environment. Smoking, for example, is not forbidden in many homes and certainly is not an activity which attracts any attention on the streets or in other public places.

The rate of suspension from the three junior high schools was higher than that in the two larger high schools in Middle City. In Rural Place, more suspensions were of students in grades seven through nine. The higher level of suspensions in these grades can be attributed to two factors--junior high students are more likely to be caught breaking rules and junior high principals are more likely to use suspension as a penalty. Junior high students are more likely to attempt to smoke in school buildings and are more likely to be caught when they do. While cutting classes and not coming to school altogether increase grade by grade, with twelfth graders the most common offenders, seventh and eighth graders are more likely to be caught and suspended for these offenses. Suspension of students at the high school level occurred more frequently for more violent offenses or for a greater accumulation of minor offenses. All other things being equal, junior high students were more likely to be suspended for rule infractions.

Two of the three junior high schools also had "automatic" suspension policies instituted by their principals. In both, smoking resulted in an automatic suspension. In one of the two, throwing snowballs also resulted in suspension. The latter rule was enacted by the principal who had faced numerous complaints from passing motorists and from school bus drivers, whose vehicles offered an apparently irresistible yellow target. The principal found that the clearly stated policy had worked to eliminate a problem which he had found difficult during the long Wisconsin winter. The smoking suspension policy, on the other hand, did not appear to be particularly successful. School discipline records showed no difference in the rate of student smokers apprehended in the two schools with the automatic suspension policy and the one without the policy. This observation might be explained either by the persistence of junior high smokers or by the fact that the percentage of students apprehended for smoking was too low for the penalty to serve as an adequate deterrent.

Both automatic suspension and the use of suspension in individual cases are discretionary decisions made by principals or assistant principals. One junior high principal did

not use suspension at all. He felt that it didn't work, that
it provided students with "a vacation," and parents of suspended students wouldn't "help discipline" so that sending
the students home would not be effective. And in some
cases there was no parent at home during the day at all. In
any event, this principal employed only "in-school solu-
tions." There was no apparent difference in the rate of rule
infractions between the schools which used suspension and
the one which did not.

Even principals who used suspension regularly were not
sure that the penalty "worked." As one put it, "Suspension
can serve a constructive function but I'm not sure it does in
all cases. It can remove a student from a situation which is
deteriorating rapidly, like when two students are feuding.
It doesn't do much for involving parents since most parents
of suspended kids don't care anyway." "But," the principal
added, "suspension can do a lot for teacher morale." At
least some teachers saw suspension as "backing them up"
and expected principals to use the penalty. Some suspensions, then, were given by principals to satisfy teacher
demands rather than to serve any purpose related to the
student rule-breaker. Suspensions are evidence for teachers
and for more distant school board members that principals
are "doing their job."

There was little agreement among teachers concerning
the larger purpose served by school suspension. While
teachers, as seen in Table 6-1, most frequently saw "involving the parents" as suspension's most important function,
there was little conviction expressed by the same teachers
during the project interviews that suspension actually served

Table 6-1

Teachers' Perceptions of Purpose of Suspension

Get Parents Involved	37.1%
Deter Student From Misbehaving	18.5
Remove Disruptive Student	17.6
Set Example for Other Students	4.4
Punish the Student	2.4
Other	1.5
More Than One Response	18.5
	100.0%

(N = 205)

that purpose. One teacher who favored the use of suspension could only think of one instance when suspension
"involved the parents." In that case, a mother made her
daughter "do housework all day long." And, the teacher
added, "That was a great penalty. The girl never caused
us any more trouble." Teachers universally saw suspension
as appropriate when the offending student was "dangerous"
or threatening other students, but these instances were relatively rare.

Teachers were also divided in their opinions about the
frequency with which suspension ought to be used as a penalty. Some teachers felt suspension ought to be used more
widely. While 20.2% of the 202 teachers responding were in
this category, 47.3% thought current rate of suspension was
"about right" and 8.9% thought suspension was used exces-
sively; 23.6% had no opinion.

Principals also talked about the "shock value" of the
first suspension. The initial suspension served as a warning
to the student and to parents that the student had been in
serious trouble. The "shock" was lessened, however, when
parents disagreed with the penalty or the rule which had
been violated. This sometimes occurred with the automatic
suspension of students for smoking, when the parents had
consented to smoking in the home.

Student Perspectives on Suspensions. Students who
had been suspended were interviewed and described the
effect of the first suspension on them. In general, the students discovered that suspension was "not so bad." Some
enjoyed the experience and the time off from school; this
group learned that suspension was not an experience to be
avoided. They talked of playing pinball on their "time off"
or of meeting friends in homes where parents were absent.
They shared the experience with their friends and boasted
of the exploits which led to their exclusion. For this group,
suspension had lost its deterrent value and even became
something to be sought. One student, a 14-year-old eighth
grader, described her suspension experience as follows:

> I was smoking in the girls' room and Mrs. ____
> caught me. ____ [the assistant principal] sus-
> pended me for three days because it was my
> second time. It was no big deal. We [her
> friends] laughed about it a lot. . . . I slept late
> each day. I went shopping with Mom and went
> to Helen's house in the afternoon. She took the
> afternoon off and we listened to records. We all
> thought the suspension was dumb.

Not all students are suspended for the three-day maximum period allowable under Wisconsin law.[33] Some were re-
admitted the next morning and others were allowed to return

to school as soon as they brought a parent to talk with the principal about the offense. None of the students interviewed reported being denied admittance at the end of the three-day period. No student was suspended without his or her parent being informed, usually by telephone. Generally students were kept in the principal's office until the end of the school day and then not allowed to return the next day. In some cases, students who were being suspended were taken to the door of the school and were thrown out by the principal.

Only half of the students who were suspended (64 of 128) responded that they had been given "a chance to tell their side of the story" before being excluded from school. The Goss decision, of course, requires that students averring innocence be afforded this opportunity. Before concluding, however, that 50% of the students were denied Court-mandated rights, it is necessary to consider how the students looked at the circumstances surrounding their meeting with the principal or vice-principal when they were suspended. In many instances the students reported that their point of view wasn't seriously considered. And that was how these students viewed "telling their side of the story." As one student put it, "He [the principal] just sat there. I might as well have been talking to his desk. He didn't pay any attention and when I was finished he suspended me anyway." Goss requires that the student be given the chance to deny the offense but doesn't require that the student's point of view be accorded equal weight with that of the person making the complaint. In addition, only those students denying their guilt must be afforded the right to talk about the offense. Order in the suspension process, then, is the value which is maximized by principals. Students about to be suspended are seldom treated as individuals.

Beyond the suspension itself, students were not allowed to make up work they missed while they were suspended from school. This policy runs counter to the Wisconsin Statute on suspensions, as detailed by the Wisconsin Department of Public Instruction.[34] No one in the schools, however, seemed to be aware of the statute. School administrators saw the lack of an opportunity to make up work as adding "teeth" to suspension as a penalty, though it was seldom mentioned by the students who were suspended. In practice, some teachers would allow students to make up work and others would give zeroes for missed tests, so the actual effect of a suspension depended substantially on the teachers who were assigned to the student.

Overall, the suspension of students from the schools was a routine occurrence. Students were afforded the opportunity to tell their side of the story but this had no influence on the outcome of individual suspension cases. Suspension, instead, depended on the individual attitudes of administrators and the specifics of individual cases, including the force with which the teacher asked for exclusion. Administrators faced strong pressure from some teachers to demonstrate "they were doing their job," as measured by suspension. Suspensions, then, are totally embedded in the sociology of the schools; the roles played by or expected of principals determine the process. Principals do not act as independent adjudicators.

Suspended students rarely denied they were engaged in the rule-breaking behavior which led to their suspension. Because almost all of these students had relatively long records of rule infractions, however, the students were often at a loss to explain why this particular event resulted in their suspension. They frequently expressed surprise that suspension was the penalty for the rule they had broken. For the suspended student, the time off from school was not onerous nor did it lead, in their estimation, to further "trouble" from school officials. It should be added that minority students were not present in large numbers in the schools which were the subjects for the research and that, therefore, statements that suspensions were sometimes racially motivated could not be tested.

The debate concerning suspension has focused on a number of other issues which can now be addressed. Those favoring more due process in this area describe the impact which suspension has on students, the possibility of mistaken suspensions, and its abuse as a penalty. We found suspension having little effect on students; in fact, students sometimes welcomed the time off. There was substantial disagreement among administrators about the penalty; some believed in it, some did not, and others used it in some cases, depending on their personal view of its effectiveness. While "mistakes" might be possible, none was observed or reported by students.

Suspension standards are highly subjective, apart from occasional policies that suspension would automatically follow from the breaking of certain rules. In only rare instances did suspension appear to serve either as a deterrent to further misbehavior or to "involve parents," its most frequently offered purpose. In sum, the debate over suspensions, both in Goss and in the education literature, is far removed from the realities of its use as a penalty. The total discipline system is at times random and unfair, but suspension is only a small part of the system. From a civil liberties perspective, random teacher discipline, some of which leads to suspension, is a larger issue.

Attention given suspensions has led principals to an increasing dependence on alternative penalties. Rural Place, for example, had a modest rate of external suspensions from school because in-school suspensions were employed. A windowless room, called "the hole" by students, was used to confine students during the hours in which the school was open. Students in the hole were closely supervised and engaged in school work as selected by their teachers. They did not, however, leave the suspension room except to eat lunch apart from other students at a separate lunch period. School officials did not feel obliged to follow either state suspension laws or court decisions in the assignment of students to the hole, since they interpreted these as related only to external suspensions. Thus students could receive terms there in excess of the three-day limit set by Wisconsin law. The other five schools were in the process of establishing in-school detention rooms at the time the research in Middle City was finishing. In-school suspensions, with more informal conditions, had been present for some time in these schools, however.

Expulsion from school requires full due process. To avoid this there has been an increased use of exemptions in the schools we studied. Unlike expulsion, which does not relieve the schools from their obligation under Wisconsin law to provide students with home-bound instruction, exemption relieves the school of all responsibility for the student. Exemption is governed by Wisconsin state statute and allows students between the ages of 16 and 18 to withdraw voluntarily from school with the consent of both parents and school officials. Each party signs a form which removes the obligation of the student to meet state attendance laws. Principals use exemption as an alternative to expulsion which requires the filing of charges, maintenance of a record, and a hearing by the school board. Several hundred parents each year sign such forms in Middle City.

Who Is Suspended? Whether a student is suspended or not depends on a number of situational variables, such as the policies and practices of individual teachers and principals. Those students who are suspended, however, are unlike their classmates in a number of respects. For the student, suspension is strongly related to other instances of rule-breaking, beyond the event which led to the suspension. Of those students who reported being suspended at least once, 79.8% indicated that they had also cut a class; 72.7% had skipped school; 73.7% had been kicked out of a class by a teacher for committing a classroom offense; and 67.7% had been assigned to detention at least once. None of the students who had been suspended reported being free of all these violations. In short, suspended students reported a very high level of involvement with the school disciplinary system aside from the offense for which they had been suspended.

An examination of informal school records showed that about three-quarters of those suspended were punished in some fashion for a subsequent rule violation within a month's time. Most of these subsequent penalties did not involve suspension. This suggests that suspension is not a great deterrent to subsequent misbehavior.

Table 6-2

Comparison of Post-High School Plans

Nonsuspended Students

| | Grades | | |
	7 - 8	9 - 10	11 - 12
College	52.4%	47.4%	40.4%
Tech School	6.8	19.3	26.2
Armed Forces	9.6	7.6	6.7
Job	20.0	18.8	22.2
Other	11.1	6.8	4.5
	99.9%	99.9%	100.0%
	N = 395	N = 367	N = 446

Suspended Students

| | Grades | | |
	7 - 8	9 - 10	11 - 12
College	31.8%	18.2%	12.5%
Tech School	0.0	12.1	22.5
Armed Forces	9.1	12.1	12.5
Job	36.4	48.5	40.0
Other	22.7	9.1	12.5
	100.0%	100.0%	100.0%
	N = 22	N = 33	N = 40

Suspended students were much less likely to see themselves as potential college students. As seen in Table 6-2, the largest group in each of three grade levels of the student sample (N = 1208) lists college attendance as their post-high school intention. Plans to attend technical school increased with grade level, and college aspirations decreased. The comparison of the whole sample with the suspended group shows significant difference in postsecondary school plans. While two-thirds of the nonsuspended group contemplates attending some school after high school graduation,

only a little over a third of those suspended have such
plans.
  Teachers and administrators were aware of the fact that
many suspended students would prefer to drop out of school
were it not for compulsory attendance laws.[35]   School personnel frequently expressed the sentiment that they were
expected to teach students who "didn't want to learn" and
that their position was more comparable to that of a reform
school house parent than to that of a teacher.   This sentiment was combined with the feeling that the teacher's role as
a professional precluded a large role in the discipline
process.   Teachers frequently stated that "my job is to
teach, not to babysit or control kids."   Teachers did not see
a failure of their curriculum or teaching practices as being
associated with student dissatisfaction.

C. Teachers' Views of the Courts

  Teachers reported that "the courts" were robbing
teachers and administrators of the opportunity to discipline
students the way they once did.   This attitude was widely
held and was expressed both by teachers with extensive
teaching experience and by those who were new to the profession.   In other words, the attitude had become part of
the teachers' mutually held perspective of the job they held.
  "Too much interference from courts" was seen as a very
important cause of school discipline problems by 44.5% of the
teacher survey respondents and as not important by 33.5%.
On another item, 59.4% of the 207 teachers responding
agreed with the statement that "teachers and administrators
have been hampered by court decisions in their application
of discipline."   A smaller percentage, 42.0%, agreed that
"administrators now have a formal process for suspending
students which enables them to better handle discipline
problems."   And about a third, 34.8% of the teachers, felt
the student "has been protected from officials' arbitrary decisions," while 25.1% admitted they "weren't sure" about the
effect of court decisions.   Thus, while some uncertainty and
mutually conflicting sentiments are present, about two-thirds
of teachers were not favorably disposed towards court
involvement in discipline matters.
  As the statements by teachers at the start of this chapter suggested, however, teachers did not often have a
terribly clear picture of what the courts actually had said
about school discipline.   Teachers often combined bits and
pieces of different decisions which they had gleaned from the
mass media in forming their impression of what "the courts"
had done.   Thus suits involving the effectiveness of schools,

such as those brought by high school graduates who can't read and the school busing cases and debate, were combined with highly publicized civil actions against a teacher which might have been reported in a teacher association journal. This melange of court decisions and individual civil cases were combined to form a general attitude on the part of many teachers that they "might be sued" and that their personal actions were threatened with imminent court review. In part, then, "the courts" seemed to serve as a convenient scapegoat and an alibi for teachers who wanted less involvement with school discipline, and in part there appeared to be genuine confusion about what the courts had done.

On the teacher survey, respondents were asked eleven true-false-not sure questions concerning major Supreme Court school discipline decisions and Wisconsin state statutes related to discipline. The questions were not designed to address obscure parts of those decisions; rather they attempted to test understanding of the principal message for teachers contained in the statute or decision. A majority of the teachers knew the correct response to five of the eleven questions. Teachers were only somewhat more likely to know the answer to questions directly related to teacher behavior than to several general questions which also involved administrators.

Several of the questions tested understanding of the Goss decision. Almost two years to the day since the decision was handed down, a bare majority, 53.6% of the 206 respondents, knew that the student had a right to a hearing before a short suspension; 27.1% thought students lacked such a right; and 19.3% weren't sure. Teachers thought the Supreme Court had gone further than it actually had in this area, a pattern repeated on other questions. Most teachers, 52.7%, incorrectly thought students had the right to legal counsel before being suspended while 12.1% disagreed and 35.3% weren't sure.

Several of the questions related to state statutes dealing with exclusionary discipline. Only a small percentage, 17.9%, responded that students could not be suspended for truancy, the interpretation of the Wisconsin attendance law made by the Wisconsin Department of Public Instruction. A mere 1.9% knew that state law limited suspensions to three days, even if parents had not talked with school administrators about the suspension. Most teachers, 63.9%, knew that teachers had no individual power to expel a student from school, though it might have been expected that a higher percentage of teachers would know they lacked the prerogative.

The feeling that the courts had gone "too far," then, was based on a substantial misunderstanding of specific

decisions and statutes.[36]   Teachers thought the courts had
entered a variety of areas where no decision at all had been
rendered and saw due process as more complete in exclusion
cases than the skeletal due process afforded by Goss.   An
unanticipated consequence, then, of increased litigation in
the education area has been the feeling on the part of
teachers that their behavior has been more substantially
circumscribed than is actually the case.

The feeling that "the courts" were a threat to the
individual teacher was also frequently expressed during the
teacher interviews.   Teachers who had never personally been
involved in court cases and who had never known a teacher
who had been involved felt threatened by lawsuit.[37]   The
sense that they might be sued was translated into two
related teacher behavior changes.   Classroom teachers
reported that they were far less physical in their dealings
with students than they used to be, and they also reported
they wanted to have much less to do with school discipline
generally.   The feeling that they wanted "out of discipline"
was enhanced by local teacher union activities.   Union
leaders had been trying in Middle City, unsuccessfully, to
have language placed in the union contract which would
relieve teachers of some obligation to spend time in halls and
washrooms where many discipline problems occur.   Union
bargaining language included vague statements about teacher
liability and may have increased teacher concern in this
area.

The decline of physical punishment was most frequently
cited by teachers when they were asked in interviews
whether their behavior was changed as a result of court
decisions.   Once they warmed to the task, teachers were
quite open about demonstrating the physical punishment
which they used to employ.   Most such activity occurred
with smaller students and at the junior high school level and
appeared less frequently as students increased in physical
stature.   Teachers reported they used physical punishment
only occasionally, and many stated that a few such
demonstrations early in the semester were usually enough to
show that the teacher was serious about classroom discipline.
One junior high math teacher reported that a quick flip of
his meter stick was a useful technique while a junior high
language teacher favored pulling the short hairs on the back
of students' necks as a punishment.

A junior high English teacher, a veteran of 25 years in
the classroom, offered observations on physical punishment
of students similar to many which were expressed.   She
said, "Discipline is handled completely differently than it
used to be.   I've let up now with the coming of the student
rights bit.   Before, when a student acted up, a slap used to

work wonders. Now I don't even nudge kids without worrying about lawsuits. I still hit them once in a while but I've mellowed a lot when it comes to physical punishment." Other teachers also indicated they still used physical punishment, which was, by the way, prohibited by local school board policies (and had been for some time), though they were more "careful." One teacher took students into the hall for "punishment" where there "aren't any witnesses."

Not all teachers were sorry to see reduced dependence on physical punishment. One teacher who had been in the same school for eleven years found that he didn't have to hit students at all. He said, "I was uncertain at first, but thought I'd follow the [school] board policy. It takes more work, but I think I'm a better teacher now that I don't have to use physical punishment." Some teachers, of course, reported that they never did strike students and "never had to." Teachers, generally, did not discuss discipline techniques with administrators. Such a discussion might be seen as an admission that the teacher had "problems with discipline" and would run counter to the norm in the schools we studied that having this problem was a sign of teacher weakness.

Summary: More Formal Procedures. The response to increased due process litigation in school discipline should be seen from several different perspectives. While the literature has assumed that what the Supreme Court has said would be understood at the local level, in fact the intended message was hardly received at all. This is not to say that Goss and other discipline decisions were ignored. Instead, they were exaggerated and contributed to the general feeling that "the courts" were greatly interfering with the running of the schools, in spite of the very narrow decisions and the deference to school administrators displayed in the Court's opinions. This exaggeration served the purpose of allowing some teachers and administrators to worry less about discipline, with the courts serving as an alibi.

At the same time, teachers and administrators sought alternatives to suspension, relying on such techniques as exemption and in-school suspension. These penalties themselves raise numerous, as yet unanswered questions, from both legal and educational perspectives. Traditional discussion of Goss then, which focused on potential harm of suspension for the student, or on increased formalism, missed the point because they failed to consider how Goss was received at the local level.

Suspensions were seldom meted out for clearly defined rule violations. Their use was a highly subjective choice, based largely on the attitude of administrators, at times governed by the need for an administrator to "prove" he or she was "doing the job." Under these circumstances there was no pattern to its use and therefore little expectation on the part of students that certain behavior would lead to suspension. This eroded the modest deterrent value to subsequent misbehavior which the penalty might have had.

Debate on formalism in school justice systems, then, ought to be submerged into the larger and more central question of the whole rule-penalty system which operates in the schools. The purposes, nature and content of rules need examination. After such questioning, rule violations and penalties could then be addressed. And to the extent that most rule violations are committed by students who have little stated interest in being in the school in the first place, greater attention should be paid to the question of how schools can make their curriculum meaningful for students who are substantially alienated from the system and to the issue of whether such children should be required to be in school in the first place.

NOTES

[1]Expulsion requires full due process -- attorneys, transcripts, and so forth -- and therefore is rarely sought in Wisconsin. The discussion in the chapter, then, focuses on the most severe penalty actually employed in Middle City and Rural Place, not on expulsions or exemptions.

[2]419 U.S. 565 (1975), at 569. This has been interpreted by an HEW publication, "Your Legal Rights and Responsibilities: A Guide for Public School Students" (OHDS 78-260481) to mean the student must be told the rule which was broken or that the administrator should write down the rule and give it to the student (page 7).

[3]Ibid., at 582.

[4]Ibid., at 573.

[5]Ibid., at 575.

[6]Ibid., at 583.

[7]Ibid., at 596.

[8]Ibid., at 595.

[9] *Tinker v. Des Moines School District*, 393 U.S. 503 (1969).

[10] *Ibid.*, at 526.

[11] *Dixon v. Alabama State Board of Education*, 294 F. 2d 150 (5th Cir.); Cert. denied, 368 U.S. 930 (1961), at 160.

[12] *Ingraham v. Wright*, 430 U.S. 651 (1977).

[13] *Ibid.*, at 682.

[14] *Ibid.*, at 681-682.

[15] *Carey v. Piphus*, 435 U.S. 247 (1978).

[16] See J. Harvie Wilkinson III, "Goss v. Lopez: The Supreme Court as School Superintendent," in Philip B. Kurland, ed., *1975 Supreme Court Review* (Chicago: University of Chicago Press, 1976). For a more reasoned view of the case, written shortly after it was decided, see Robert E. Phay, "1975 Student Discipline Decisions by the United States Supreme Court," *New Directions in School Law* (Topeka: National Organization on Legal Problems in Education, 1976), p. 69.

[17] David L. Kirp, "Proceduralism and Bureaucracy: Due Process in the School Setting," 28 *Stanford Law Review* 841 (1976).

[18] Burton B. Goldstein, Jr., "Due Process in the Public Schools--An Analysis of the Procedural Requirements and a Proposal for Implementing Them," 54 *North Carolina Law Review* 641 (1976).

[19] In the only pre-Goss suspension study, which formed part of an amicus brief in the case, the Children's Defense Fund had looked at what it considered "excessive" use of school suspensions and at the disproportionate suspension of minority students, using Office of Civil Rights data. See Children's Defense Fund, *School Suspensions* (Washington, D.C.: The Washington Research Project, Inc., 1975).

[20] See "Student Wrongs Versus Student Rights," *Nation's Schools and Colleges*, April, 1975.

[21] Michael L. Berger, *Violence in the Schools: Causes and Remedies* (Bloomington: Phi Delta Kappa Educational Foundation, 1974).

[22]Gerald R. Bocciardi, "Suspensions: The Approach Positive," 38 Journal of Secondary Education 7 (1963), p. 64.

[23]William P. Strunk, "Exclusion from School as a Disciplinary Tool" (Washington: National Association of Secondary School Principals, 1961), p. 140.

[24]Children's Defense Fund, Children Out of School in America (Washington: The Washington Research Report, Inc., 1974), p. 121.

[25]John J. Stretch and Philip E. Crunk, "School Suspension: Help or Hindrance?" in Rosemary Sari and Frank E. Maple, eds., The School in the Community (Washington: National Association of Social Workers, 1972).

[26]Patricia Lines, "The Case Against Short Suspensions," 12 Inequality in Education 41 (July, 1972).

[27]Children's Defense Fund, School Suspensions, op cit., p. 50.

[28]Charles A. Reich, The Greening of America (New York: Bantam Books, 1970), p. 149.

[29]J. F. Feldhusen, "A Longitudinal Study of the Correlates of Children's Social Behavior" (Bethesda, Md.: ERIC Document ED079634, 1973).

[30]Southern Regional Council and the Robert F. Kennedy Memorial, The Student Pushout (Washington: SRC and RFK Memorial, 1973).

[31]Most of these related to insubordination or other instances when students challenged the authority of teachers or administrators.

[32]See fn. 19 supra.

[33]Wis Stat. § 120.13 (1) (1981).

[34]Wisconsin Statutes §120.13(1)(b)(1981) states, "The school must follow procedures which (4) Provide the students with an opportunity to take any quarterly, semester, or grading period examination missed during the suspension period."

[35]Students in Wisconsin were required to remain in school until the end of the semester in which they became 18, if the school district had a vocational, technical or adult educational institution within its boundaries and until the end of the semester in which the student became 16, if the district did not have such an institution. In effect, this made it easier for rural students to drop out of school, since many rural areas did not have VTAE institutions. This law was repealed in 1981.

[36]There is a large "impact" literature which discusses how court decisions are understood, misunderstood, and received generally by the public. As might be expected, distortion is more the rule than the exception. See, for example, "Public Response to the Court," which is Chapter 2, in Kenneth M. Dolbeare and Phillip E. Hammond's, The School Prayer Decisions (Chicago: University of Chicago Press, 1971). On page 15 of that chapter, Dolbeare and Hammond reprint part of a 1966 Wisconsin Survey Research Laboratory poll of Wisconsin adults. At that time, a majority of respondents did not know the Supreme Court had made decisions in "recent years" on the rights of defendants accused of crimes or on redistricting of state legislatures. As in many areas of political activity, many people have strong feelings about the Court and Court decisions without specific information.

[37]In the two school districts under study, central administrators could recall only two suits, both involving the same teacher, in the previous ten years. There was no wave of lawsuits swamping the schools in these two Wisconsin communities.

Chapter 7

APPROACHES TO BETTER SCHOOL DISCIPLINE

Question: What is your philosophy of education?
Answer: [By principal] Clean up our own house
              first. There is no way the school can yell
              at the students until we make sure that we
              are providing them with the services they
              need. What we need is a broad-based
              curriculum with alternatives to meet each
              individual's needs.
Question: What do you see as the purpose of
              discipline in the school?
Answer: To make the job of teaching possible, to
              make it possible for all students to learn.
              Discipline is a maturing process, in that it
              allows the individual to think and act and
              move forward.
Question: How does your own approach to discipline
              differ from that of others in the school?
Answer: Many people in the school think I am too
              soft. I think that is because they don't
              see the total picture. They may forget
              why they're here and get too concerned
              about taking stronger actions. But some-
              times you just can't do it. Some staff
              would like more dramatic action, like
              throwing the kid out of school. But to do
              this would just result in the kid's coming
              back to haunt the school.
Question: What is your role in the discipline process?
Answer: I see myself as the second or third stage
              in the disciplinary process. I am the

133

Question:

Answer:

Question:

Answer:

Question:

Answer:

evaluator of a situation that has arisen. I can relieve others if their emotions have carried them away. I guess my job is to distill the situation and come up with answers if I can.

How much time do you devote to disciplinary matters?

Everything I do deals indirectly with discipline. In terms of direct contact with discipline, probably 15%.

What is the role of others in the process?

Teachers must be professionally prepared and able to project a mastery in their subject area. Teaching is important. An interesting class could mean fewer discipline problems. Also teachers need to be interested in one another and in the school. Not too many with tunnel vision. Few of the teachers restrict themselves to their own classroom these days. Five or six years ago, several teachers took the attitude that they could handle things however they wanted to in their classrooms, and had no responsibilities outside their rooms. But that has changed. Students see the teachers talking to one another, getting along in the halls and around the school. And they say to themselves, "Hey, this is a pretty nice place; this school is OK. People care." And then students care, too.

How could handling discipline be improved?

One way would be for us to know our roles better. We must provide more alternatives: alternative schools; more specialists available; full-time behavioral disabilities teachers; psychologists, social workers, behavior modifications groups; better communications with other institutions. There are a thousand various agencies--such as churches--that we could use.

A. Overview and Review

Our empirical findings describe a very discretionary discipline system based on surprisingly little agreement about

desired goals and practices and on widely shared myths
about the origin of school discipline problems. Discipline is
integrated with the whole of the schooling enterprise.
Events and relationships nominally having to do with discipline are actually related to the psychosocial outlooks of
teachers and administrators, and their views of the general
goals and structure of education. More specifically, we have
found the following:

1) Discipline problems in the Middle-American schools
   we studied do not threaten the social control of
   the school. Attendance violations and liquor-drug
   problems are present often enough to cause concern, but for the most part everyday misbehaviors
   involve minor squabbling and deviance.

2) There is a great deal of "slippage" in the system,
   since enforcement is very decentralized. Teachers
   vary in their perceptions of misbehavior, their
   orientations toward punishment, and their desire to
   be actively involved. Lots of misbehaviors are
   undetected, and most of those detected are not
   punished.

3) Although students and teachers alike believe the
   discipline system to be very fair, both believe
   (correctly) that high achievers in school are
   favored when discipline issues arise. That high
   achievers are caught less when they misbehave,
   and are punished less even when they misbehave
   frequently, represents a form of discrimination.

4) Stereotypical background variables often thought
   to explain misbehavior are related only very
   modestly to discipline problems, but student self
   expectations and relationship to the curriculum are
   very important in explaining repeated misbehavior.

5) The sanctions the school uses for student misbehavior are not imposed systematically, and often
   their use seems more counterproductive than
   effective.

6) Schools lack factual information about the origins
   of discipline problems and create myths about the
   origins of school disorder which relate to the social
   class characteristics of students.

7) School personnel react with hostility to the efforts
   by courts (and other central government agencies)
   to take a role in school conduct. The nature and
   scale of court activity is perceived in a distorted
   and inaccurate manner.

These findings, drawn from Chapters 3-6, relate to one
another. For example, the noncrisis aspect of the disciplinary climate in the schools helps to permit a discretionary

system to dominate over an alternative approach emphasizing strictness and accountability. The discretionary system permits the high achiever to secure preferred treatment, the teacher to commute psychosocial preferences into apprehension and penalty, and a kind of crazy-quilt imposition of serious penalties like home suspensions by administrators.

As we indicated in Chapter 2, our preferred standard in evaluating the dynamics of discipline is that there be as much student autonomy permitted as is consonant with the school's need for order. Moreover, schools should seek optimal positions on an autonomy and order curve. Given these guidelines, we turn in the section that follows to a detailed evaluation of the discipline practices.

B. Discipline in Schools: An Evaluation

When one considers the educational goals of most secondary schools, the need for balancing autonomy and order, and the available resources, it seems on balance that the schools in this study have devised policies and practices which blend educational goals and discipline in a generally suitable fashion. Of course, school discipline practices are not static and we found evidence that there has been and will be incremental change and evolution of policies and procedures.

At the extremes, however, there is behavior which is not acceptable, judged by educational goals or standards of fairness. While the overall pattern described in earlier chapters is satisfactory, there are areas of fault. These, not just the troubled students, are discipline problems of the school. There are areas in which schools do not consistently base decisions and policies on empirical information blended with educational goals and organizational needs.

Two Instances of Successful Problem Handling: Differences in Classroom Management and Attention to Order-Keeping. In considering the success of schools in addressing discipline problems, we were initially confronted with teachers who have markedly different approaches to general classroom organization. Although such diversity might cause serious problems (in other schools or at another time), in these schools differences in classroom management were not a problem. Teachers handle their classrooms in many varied ways, both academically and socially. They have distinctly personal ways to diagnose and cope with social behaviors. For students, such differences in style impose the responsibility of learning the behavioral expectations of their teachers; this they accomplish in the first few days of a school term. There is no reason, in the name of educational goals or fairness or autonomy for students, to reduce such diversity of style. Indeed, such diversity reflects some of our expectations about education. Most of us would agree that there is no one sure or best way for a teacher to teach, and that a good teacher may be either strict or permissive, direct or "laid back." Since schools have strong traditions about the autonomy of teachers in classrooms, attempts to "iron out" differences in practice would be resisted mightily.

Outside the individual classrooms, the need of schools for order requires shared expectations for behavior in public spaces. Such understanding is preferred by all to a totally unstructured situation. Schools develop rules, varying in nature from formal to informal, for their congregate spaces and situations. Teachers have rather diverse expectations about the meaning and enforcement of those rules. The application of these rules, as we have seen, is sometimes uncomfortable for teachers, inasmuch as they would prefer others to handle misbehavior in these areas according to personal taste and style.

At the extremes very great differences in teacher behavior in both classroom and public area management are not acceptable. That a teacher should use minor corporal punishment (not to mention major corporal punishment) in a school having policies against corporal punishment is unacceptable. Teacher styles so diverse as to permit extreme student behavior also are not acceptable. Schools, with their shared expectations of teacher and student behavior, usually tolerate diversity so long as it falls within the framework of common rules or practices. Teacher differences in style were not a serious problem in the secondary schools in this study, although among teachers there is some discomfort over such differences.

A second kind of school problem that has been handled adequately is order-keeping. Schools spend a lot of time keeping order and a certain degree of order is necessary for them to function. Much of society prizes order in schools, even though the reasons for the esteem accorded it are not clear. Most teachers and administrators also seem to think they cannot function without a considerable degree of order around them, though our research has shown that there are differences in the amount teachers require. Some devote time and energy to order maintenance as a major activity. Others try to avoid a role in order maintenance altogether.

When order-keeping is carried to extremes, such as requiring rule-breakers to do a large number of pushups, or extending the zone of order for blocks around the school, it becomes questionable whether educationally oriented order-keeping has been replaced by the pursuit of order-keeping

for its own sake. Since out-of-class order-keeping is primarily delegated to principals and assistant principals,
extremes in order-keeping usually can be attributed to a new
initiative by administrators. The possibilities that a school
will become obsessed with order must be taken seriously
because such efforts to attain order can ultimately damage
the school.

If school personnel find themselves spending a lot of
time enforcing rules, such time expenditure should be the
cue for examining whether the rules are worth the effort.
In some instances, schools have reasoned by analogy to the
criminal justice system and found that their rules can be
simplified, pared down, or even thrown out. Dress code
rules, once very common, were retired in most schools after
efforts to enforce them became very time costly and teachers
began to question why they were spending so much time
reporting dress violations and thinking up appropriate
punishments. The whole motive for dress codes was
reviewed. To what extent did they have an educationally
justifiable purpose, and to what extent did enforcement
require more resources than seemed sensible? Were they
disruptive of educational order?

Both order-keeping and differences in classroom
management in the schools we studied are expressed in
acceptable and appropriate ways, for the most part. Neither
problem is permanently "solved" in the schools, but both are
"solved" in the sense that a reasonable balance currently
exists between educational objectives and school responses.
There may be marginal practices by some individuals, but
overall a kind of reasonable balance exists in classroom
management and order-keeping between the needs of
students for development and of the school for continuity
and uniformity.

Serious Discipline Problems in Schools. There are,
however, serious problems having to do with discipline
issues in these schools. Some of the problems are more
acute in one of the schools than in others, but all suffer
from the same general problems. These problems are serious
in the sense that their existence inhibits the ability of the
school to function efficiently; these problems keep the school
from maximizing student and staff autonomy while keeping
order. Often these problems are hard to specify and even
harder to address, in that they overlap and reinforce one
another.

The schools discussed in this book did have
problems--problems which could be solved with information
and imagination and problems which were rather different in
scope from the ones they thought they had.

1.   Discrimination.   Discrimination   in   schools
serves no legitimate educational purpose and is clearly con-
trary to the principles of administrative justice.   In the
schools studied there were various aspects of discrimination
that are of concern.   Our data do not speak to the issue of
racial discrimination because the minority population in each
school was very small.   They do speak to the question of
whether other background variables, essentially beyond the
control of the student, directly influence how he or she
fares in the discipline system.   They reveal some modest
problems   of   discrimination   against   males   and   somewhat
stronger   discrimination   in   favor   of   upper-middle-class
students.   But the main discrimination shown through the
empirical indicators is discrimination in favor of those who
are   in-school   achievers.   High-grade,   high-achievement
students are treated much more lightly when they do break
school   rules,   controlling   for   frequency   of   rule-breaking.
Students who are involved in extracurricular activities also
enjoy some favorable discrimination.   Discrimination in favor
of achievers is, of course, very common in organizations.
However, for a school with large numbers of other benefits
available to achievers (class office, honor society), there
seems no reason to exempt good students from punishments
they deserve, if less academically achieving students incur
them.   In   addition,   there   is   some   evidence   that
low-achievement students respond to this discrimination with
retaliatory subsequent rule-breaking.

A more subtle kind of discrimination is found in the
whole upper-middle-class tone of the high schools in this
study.   The upper-middle-class bias of American schooling
is, in part, built into the role orientations held by teachers
and administrators who seek to deliver children to institutions of higher education and ultimately to high-status jobs.
Equal chances to succeed or to be rewarded when showing
improvement are too often not offered to the noncollege
bound, who then act out, may incur suspensions or other
penalties, or feel so unwelcome and unintegrated that they
leave school.[2]

Some vocational courses and work-release programs were
offered in the communities we studied,   Even so, low status
continued to be attached to noncollege, nongeneral courses,
and a sizable percentage of the student body felt outside the
mainstream.   Could the schools alter this?   Recent studies
indicating that school-based vocational programs do not provide good training for actual employment and earnings raise
serious questions about ways to provide meaningful alternatives to the traditional upper-middle-class, college-oriented
programs.[3]   In upper-middle-class biased schools, quiet
noncollege-bound children are tolerated and the disciplinary

focus of the school is directed at those who are not so quiet.

The general discrimination toward upper-middle-class aspirations found in the school program has as its inevitable parallel, in these schools, rewarding of upper-middle-class high achievers. To put it another way, the discipline system, like the academic system, rewards those for whom it is designed. Different types of schools, with more program offerings and a meaningful set of classes and activities for students whose orientation is work rather than college, would be likely to keep students interested. And interested students, as numerous studies show, would be less likely to be disruptive or to drop out.[4]

2. Discipline Myth Creation. Schools are institutions in which little attention is given to information exchange among teachers and administrators. Information that is exchanged regarding discipline is usually episodic, anecdotal, and expressive. Since they are not data oriented and since their teaching staffs feel very much their "special" position, schools have considerable capacity to develop and foster aberrations about themselves. They can and do overreact to problems, exaggerate them, create fictions about themselves, and respond to those fictions. One of the schools we studied was such an organization. It responded to problems that were overdramatized and in doing so created a learning and working environment suitable for acrimony, but not education. It became a troubled school.

However alarming problems may seem, schools need to be more conscious of the amount of autonomy they do have and of their ability to change situations. If they have been prudent enough to keep simple discipline data over time, if they have some common policies with regard to rights and responsibilities, if they have some within-staff communication links, they can respond affirmatively to problems.[5] But without some infrastructure, schools can be destructive places when problems arise.

Troubles in schools, we suggest, can easily get out of hand because of the internal organization of the school and the socialization of teachers. The avoidance of such chain reaction requires the establishment of some within-school practices which are educationally sound and functional for organizational maintenance. To the extent, then, that schools lack a fail-safe plan, they are open to irrational response.

The distribution of authority in schools, with principals having so much more authority and visibility than anyone else, can also leave them very open to myths about discipline.[6] If the principal persists in saying things are badly out of hand, it is difficult to gainsay him or her.

Likewise, principals can create the impression that the discipline climate has improved. Part of the apparent success of new principals in changing school climate may be due to their monopoly in having and disseminating information about what is transpiring in "our school."

    3. Junior High Schools. Problems with the way school personnel confront discipline are seen most explicitly in the junior high school and middle school. The problems of student maturation and programming that confront such schools, with pupils caught between childhood and high school responsibilities, are unsolved. The educational psychology theorists concerned with responsibility and moral development find that such students are remarkably diverse in the degree of order needed and the responsibility they can assume. Junior high and middle schools mirror this conflict. The most common response by schools to such student diversity is to focus on order, on having many rules and emphasizing the appropriateness of learning and obeying them. Yet rules imposing external authority make some assumptions about the absence of internal sources or order, assumptions not proven or understood in the literature.

    The junior high schools we studied imposed a high degree of order. Some of the techniques employed are clearly easier to apply on physically smaller students. And challenge and disobedience can be read as calls for more order, not for less. Thus, among the schools discussed in this book, it was a junior high school which had the greatest problems and the lowest morale, and among all the junior highs there was much less sense of fairness reported by students. It was a junior high school that had the most distorted way of viewing discipline. It seems that junior high schools have been more inclined to fail to consider consciously the ways in which they characterize discipline problems and the way they look at students. Such failure has created special problems for them.

    4. Troubled Students. The problems raised by troubled students overlap very much with the problems of explicit and implicit discrimination discussed above. While some students have learning disabilities or psychological dysfunctions, troubled students in most cases simply are students who see the school program as irrelevant to their concerns. For them, classes are boring and they do not relate positively to any adult in the school.

    In response to the presence of students seemingly uninvolved in regular classes, some schools have attempted to introduce more varied programming, some have utilized more community-based work or experience programs, some have therapeutically utilized attendance waivers or exemptions, and some have good counselors. Some schools have created dropout prevention programs based on what students say is wrong with the basic school program. Others have emphasized parental involvement; still others have peer counseling or youth mediation. The list goes on and on, but the central dimension lies in the development of affirmative planning for services to the student whose goals do not include post-high school education.

The lack of strategy for working with students for whom the curriculum had no appeal was notable in the schools we studied. Obviously, having a variety of strategies does not ensure success, but the lack of attention to the disaffected student made misbehavior more likely. Blaming the student, which was cheap in the the short run, came back to haunt schools in terms of increased organized troublemaking and dropout.

Discipline Problems in Sum. As indicated earlier, the four major problems in the secondary schools studied overlap greatly. There is both beauty and despair in this overlap--the problems seem so much harder to resolve because they are overlaid. On the other hand, beginning to solve one of the problems should help with the others. Thus, for example, demythification might lead to less discrimination in program emphasis, more alternatives for previously alienated or troubled students. These four problems are all indicators that the schools are operating in suboptimal ways in terms of autonomy and order. Myths prevent rational assessment of cause and effect, and thus the needs of troubled students remain unmet. Rather than addressing problems of discrimination and bias, schools (especially junior high schools) stick to tried and true emphases, like order.

Yet, discipline problems such as these are not what they seem. They do not, as the reader has probably realized, have simple causes or lend themselves to quick remedies. A school staff cannot reasonably say "let's handle our discipline problems better" and hope in a few hours to move significantly to solve any of the four problems just identified.

These types of school problems arise in substantial part from the structure of schooling, such as the mandatory inclusion of all students, the current fashions in age grouping, and the differentiated status attached to being a principal. If not invariant, these are at least very difficult to change. The other major source of school discipline problems, aside from the structure of schools, is the nature of educational goals. These, too, have great resiliency to change. Schools have traditionally been accustomed to preparing students for postsecondary education--this has been their major goal. Thirty years of greater emphasis on nonacademic programming have not been without effect. Still, the schools we studied discriminated against those without academic aspirations or success. The students who did poorly in traditional subjects, because disillusioned with school, often turned to troublemaking.

To work successfully with the discipline problems of these schools requires being willing to consider the links between both the structure of schooling and educational goals on the one hand and discipline patterns on the other. Discipline patterns, we reiterate, are mingled with the fundamental assumptions and modes of schooling, and to change them requires a willingness to engage in serious self-study.

C.   Making Changes Affecting School Discipline

There are numerous forces insulating the school against serious change with regard to discipline. A very strong force constraining schools from altering their practices is the interconnectedness of all aspects of schooling. Schools are somewhat like the multiproblem family, in which working on any single problem may seem pointless because of the interrelatedness of all problems. One cannot release half the students in the senior class from school at noon for a semester in order to further community participation without affecting staffing patterns for the teachers, the offerings in the curriculum, the utilization of space in the school, the retention of special subjects, etc. School administrators time and time again report that their hands are tied by the age and experience of their teaching staff, by tradition, and by an array of other factors. At the same time that school administrators stress their personal flexibility and receptivity to new techniques, they indicate that their freedom is limited by numerous other parties. The school board, the courts, the staff, the parent community, and the school administration are all frequently mentioned as forces preventing more positive events at school sites.

Yet, the negative aspects of the interconnectedness of the varied aspects of schooling can be exaggerated. The literature on innovation in schools suggests that well-planned, carefully developed changes are possible if institutional interconnectedness is recognized as a source of strength rather than as a constraint. Recent activities of some schools to avoid closing, like welcoming preschools or staying in operation for twelve months a year, suggest that schools can solve problems creatively despite the many obstacles to changing directions. The critical element in using the interconnectedness of schooling rather than being defeated by it is planning how internal and external inputs will relate to the change process and the desired outputs. A kind of systems approach can be useful in conceptualizing change.

Another important obstacle to school change is the way schools look at discipline. They see it as an issue to be avoided. Often, schools look at discipline issues in we-they terms, defining discipline problems as confrontations to order raised by uncaring or possibly venal students. Issues are defined in very immediate and personal terms: "He was really nasty and vulgar to me and I won't tolerate it." Schools have little sense of the overall presence and type of problems to be confronted and have some difficulty in viewing discipline problems impersonally. Partly because of the personalized aspect of discipline, schools tend not to become involved in a serious review of discipline; it is a touchy issue and potentially an embarrassing one. Teachers tend to regard their own discipline-handling records very favorably and look with dismay on the discipline dispensed by colleagues and, to a lesser extent, principals. Because they work side by side, day after day, with the same people, they are reluctant to become involved in a systematic review of discipline, lest they embarrass fellow teachers (who may be on the same staff for twenty or thirty years) or principals (who have ultimate authority about so many things). However much teachers find fault with other teachers' handling of problems, they close ranks against most implications that the school must assume substantial responsibility for discipline problems. "It doesn't matter what we do," commented one teacher. "Kids bring their problems into the school and we have to live with them as best we can." This common view assumes that that school itself can only react to discipline problems and in no way contributes to or exacerbates them.

The personalization of discipline makes the issue sufficiently "sticky" to deal with that schools tend to opt for more mechanical approaches to problems. They tend to "add on" here and there--to try in-school suspension programs or centralized detention systems, or to close or open campuses after relatively short-term planning. These fads to address discipline and other educational problems are often adopted without much thought following their introduction elsewhere, sometimes without enough consideration as to whether the innovation is actually appropriate in the local setting. In rare times of fairly flexible school budgets, there may be money for extra staff for grounds, hall monitors, or instructional staff for in-school suspension rooms, but for the most part, schools think about discipline in the short range, with staff already in place, and uncritically adopt the ideas of others so long as they do not cause personal confrontations. Their preference is for incremental, partial measures, rather than for systemwide review and change.

Another obstacle to the solving of problems is that schools may assume that problems are inevitable. For example, it may be stated as inevitable that junior high schools or middle schools have numerous discipline problems because children are immature, have no work or program options for all practical purposes, and are extremely involved in the social context of schooling. Someone subscribing to the inevitability of junior high and middle school problems would doubt that anything could or should be done about unfairness in school discipline because certain assumptions have been made about the role of the school and the psychosocial development of children.

Moreover, schools are for the most part shielded from the competitive marketplace. They do not have to bid for grants or compete for contracts; in fact, they have little control over the budgetary aspects of their activity. Lacking budget controls and being obligated to accept whatever ages and types of students the law requires, schools exist in a monopoly situation that is not calculated to inspire self-criticism. Their traditions of monopoly and conservatism do not suit schools for organizational examination and change. The children who choose to attend private school or to relinquish schooling are sufficiently few in number that the public schools need not pay much attention to their perspectives.

The lack of demonstrable efficacy in schools also acts to inhibit the willingness to entertain new policies. Schools have rarely been able to be specific about educational techniques, objectives of schooling, or measures of organizational success. There is very little technological certainty about the process of schooling--what works best or where it will lead. School people are overall quite accustomed to an environment in which only gross performance measures seem at all salient. The number of dropouts, the number of seniors entering college--these are statistics schools understand. So are the average reading and mathematics levels for different grades and minimum competency tests for high school graduation. We recognize, however, that there is a disagreement on what a good teacher is and what the important curriculum content is for students. Similarly there is much disagreement about the best means for handling disenchanted students, whether it is to be firm or forgiving, whether to use special groups (a form of segregation) or whole school programs. Since almost none of these choices has any technological or verifiable certainty about it, schools are willing at most to try low-risk things. The net impact

of lack of demonstrable efficacy is to permit a very
traditional set of practices to continue.

The recently emergent effective schools literature represents an effort to introduce more precision into the
relationship between different aspects of school functioning
and school output. These efforts have not advanced far
enough to permit systematic evaluation of areas of
programming within the school, however.

D. Changes in Discipline

Moving from the problems identified earlier and the
general obstacles that inhibit schools from solving problems,
we now turn to the kinds of remedies which should be considered and applied. Although the constraints on making
changes are enormous, we think that schools are concerned
enough about discipline issues to be interested in exploring
options for change and to use evidence to devise rational
policy which will in broad terms express an appropriate
educational mission. To us, this implies policy choices which
permit the maximal development of autonomy with maintenance
of order, seeking the optimal blend of the two.[8]

The materials presented here are concerned both with
the general process of remedy and with specifics. Thus,
initially we turn to general suggestions about the remedy
process, to kinds of perspectives that all school-oriented
people interested in discipline policy should consider regardless of the characteristics of a particular school. Later, we
consider for the schools described in chapters 3 through 6
the kinds of remedies that are likely to be most helpful for
the problems that are most troublesome. We do this to illustrate the application of general rules, and because we
believe the "discipline problems" of these schools are pervasive in the United States.

General Rules: 1. Demythification. Many schools (and
other organizations) are handicapped in their ability to diagnose and solve problems by a set of myths. These vary
from school to school, but fairly representative myths include the idea that the kids from across the tracks are the
source of all the troublemaking, the concept that the school
is under siege from a cohort of vindictive students, the
belief that the school is powerless to change this, and the
attitude that the community or the law represents intrusive
threats which must be kept at bay. Myths, both the positive and the negative ones, tend to assume a life of their
own and to condition both short- and long-term planning and
coping. Because myths can be so widely shared and so
pervasive, it is important for schools to take stock of

whether there are discipline myths prevailing, what they are, and in what ways they inhibit problem definition and solving. Some myths are probably functional, and there is always the risk that when institutions begin to look at myths, they will shatter both the functional and dysfunctional.

2. Thinking through. In most schools, a central concept to change should be joint or mutual thinking through, as a process. Schools, with their largely pyramidal structure, are generally places in which systems of mutual reliance are strong, but mutual responsibilities and problem solving are much less common. This distribution of responsibility, though welcome in that it distributes the workload, also acts to preclude the involvement of large numbers of adults in the making of policies. Yet the policies, such as closed or open campus, modular or period time systems, are to be enforced by all the adults in the school regardless of their participation in formulating them. What is suggested here is a clearer articulation of the "jointness" of problem identification and solution, with recognition that having only the principal (or principals) handle such things is an uncreative solution that is in itself a problem. Teachers have diverse techniques, strategies, and skills which should more systematically be shared and developed as part of school policy making.

Information and perspective sharing can be carried out informally, of course, or more formally through in-service programs or workshops. Such thinking through may involve outside authorities who get discussion started or respond with special expertise to identified problems. What is important is the ability of the school as an institution to think and talk about itself, with the expectation and recognition that the school is a joint endeavor.

In some schools the development of an educational philosophy has been the beginning of such a thinking-through process; in other schools the thinking-through process has culminated with a statement of educational philosophy, which has been central to a variety of school processes (from discipline to curriculum). In other schools, the thinking-through model has taken the form of involving teachers to a greater extent with feelings of shared responsibility and authority.

3. Coordination. Coordination in the school context means the development of a generally understood and shared management plan, based on a set of rules and expectations. In most schools there is a management plan, either implicit or explicit. Frequently, the plan is not clearly articulated and not as carefully coordinated as it should be. As indicated above, although we recognize the

need for teachers to have the right to differ in styles of teaching and classroom management, we emphasize that there are limits to the ability of a school to tolerate diversity of style. If there is great diversity of style for common spaces (lunchrooms and bathrooms), there will be more problems presented. Thus, the well-functioning school must provide for a certain amount of coordination and management.

By analogy, we might ask what would happen in a family home if each person decided to be responsible only for the cleaning of his or her bedroom. We can all recognize that for the shared or public areas, there needs to be some system for coordinating the cleaning and a system for the actual cleaning. The same approach applies to the schools.

Coordination in schools may be enhanced through a variety of mechanisms. It may be developed through programs wholly within the school. Or it may profitably involve the use of outside people, whether they are "organizational doctors" or people from other schools with different experiences with coordination. Sometimes the preparation and implementation of a school code, or its revision, can be the opening wedge for better coordination.

4. The hard cases: a separate issue? In talking about remedies we need to recognize, as administrators and teachers have always done, that there are some children in school who raise problems that are almost insoluble. There are kids who set fires repeatedly, attack students or teachers, extort money, and generally induce a climate of fear. These children have been the theoretical grounds on which to base fairly harsh exclusionary discipline measures such as expulsion. Such children will continue to be present in schools, and it is important that their presence not unduly inhibit the ability of schools to respond to the majority of students. Schools need to be wary about globalizing the conduct or handling of the hard cases; they are not representative and should not be treated as such. They should not become the fulcrum for policy, nor should policies developed with reference to them be applied generally or often, unless exceptional circumstances warrant. In some schools suspensions (intended to cope with dangerous or extremely distraught students) have in the past been used for minor disciplinary infractions. Thus, a very special kind of punishment has been globalized inappropriately.

There is social-psychological evidence that the misbehaviors and crimes of youth stem from very different orientations, that some illegal activities are designed to send messages to schools, and that others represent in-school acting out of personal tensions and problems having little to do with the school itself.[9] So far as possible, schools should attempt to use staff and professional resources to make these kinds of distinctions, and then cope accordingly. Thus, for some students, a competent school psychologist working with receptive teachers may be the right resource for hard cases.

Differentiated strategies are needed to address different kinds of problems, and this area will remain a thorny one. For some kinds of difficult cases, collective responses (school moot courts and student vandalism squads) which combine social pressure with explicit rules may be effective. In other hard cases, however, the most rational and creative of schools will be unable to do anything. Alternative settings and exit seem to be all that remain, coupled with professional help as appropriate.

5.   Choice.   The element of choice is a difficult one for most schools, particularly senior high schools, which already have a great deal of choice in courses and career preparation tracks.   Many offer evening schools providing regular basic skills courses leading to general equivalent degrees as an alternative to high school graduation.   Yet, there are additional types of choice to which most schools need to give explicit attention.   In many communities there are vocational schools and colleges which are open to contracting with schools to offer services.   Through such arrangements, a student can take basic skills courses at the high school part of the day and be accepted in a short term vocational preparation course for the remainder of the day. The school incurs the costs of the contract, but is able to provide the kinds of basic skills the vocational school requires for enrollment (especially of underage youth), at the same time the student is obtaining training in an area of interest to him or her.

Alternative schools, including parochial schools, may afford students opportunities to which they can relate more affirmatively.   In larger communities, alternative schools may be part of the public schools system.   They vary from creative, independent study kinds of programs to schools created specifically for troubled youth.[10]   Still other alternatives include sabbaticals from school, more home-bound instruction possibilities, and work-counseling-study programs developed with private nonprofit groups.

The responsibility for providing information about such choices for students falls hard upon schools.   School personnel are often not knowledgeable about the resources of the community for students who seem unlikely to persist in regular public school.   Outside the school, very few communities have youth services with counselors able to explore the best-suited range of alternatives.   Other institutions, such as vocational schools, cannot usually provide staff for tailor-made programming for problematic

students.   Therefore, the student who wishes to explore
nontraditional choices is very likely to fall between the
cracks of the system.   In most communities none of the
existing systems is likely to provide a true sense of the
choices that are the best fit for students whose problems or
wishes take them outside the routine schooling channels.
Students without substantial personal skills and resources
will often be lost in the shuffle and fail to continue with
educational programming.

Within-school choices are usually reserved for the final
two high school years, with the assumption that the first two
high school years are for basic skills.   For some students
choice in academic programming may come too late if it is
reserved for juniors and seniors.   Choices need to be developed and made available earlier.

6.   Loosening up.   Over a decade ago most schools
quietly abolished dress codes rather than devote scarce resources to their enforcement.   We suggest that there may be
lessons to be learned from this experience, especially that
schools should seriously consider loosening up some of their
rules.   Rules, like myths, sometimes tend to develop lives of
their own, lives which require precious time for dubious
enforcement.   Some rules are probably eternal, but others
should be reviewed on a staff-wide basis as to their
necessity, their meaning, and the enforcement costs and
benefits.   In the criminal justice system, there has been
more interest in and experimentation with decriminalization.
The evidence on the impact of such change is not final, but
there are strong indications that when rules are relaxed,
behavior does not change markedly and staff-citizen friction
is much reduced.

Our perspective is that schools should consider how
they can provide the best blend of order and autonomy
which will result in more fairness and self-respect, for both
teachers and students.   Loosening up, giving up some vestiges of order, may be a necessary early step in implementing this perspective.

The reader will note that we have suggested fairly general approaches to change, stemming from our recognition
that problems initially appearing to be discipline in reality
stem from educational goals and the structure of schooling,
that discipline is embedded in a variety of school processes.
Thus our emphasis has been on presenting suggestions which
address not only discipline, but also educational structure
and goals.   We are not saying that modest changes have no
role.   But our study has helped to illustrate that some kinds
of changes--such as increasing the legal formalism in
discipline--will (1) do little to address the problems that are

most serious in schools and (2) probably be deflected from having much effect.[11]

Specific Remedies for Specific Problems. Our suggestions for specific policy remedies are intended both to embody the general rules just discussed and to give illustrations of appropriate school application of these general rules within the context that there are structural limits to change.

1.   Teachers differences in style. For the schools we have studied, the differences in teacher style raise problems only at the extreme. The principal in each school should be active in conveying to teachers and staff what the boundaries of acceptable differences in style are. The principal thus should convey what is not acceptable and carry out spotting and enforcing conduct which is consciously oriented to preventing damaging variations in teacher style. Principals need to be sensitive to communicating clearly what the boundaries are, how these limits may affect teacher styles, and the types of issues that get teachers into school board and court hearings. Moreover, they need to work affirmatively with school boards to have a shared sense of appropriate conduct, especially with reference to physical contact with students. As indicated earlier, such boundaries must be set with sensitivity to thinking through and coordination, not simply created by top-down action.

2.   Order-keeping. As suggested above, there is sometimes momentum in order-keeping which seems difficult to arrest. Yet there are unnecessary, sometimes high, costs to regimentation. Order-keeping in the school needs to be assessed in terms of its appropriateness to educational objectives. Order-keeping activity needs to be reviewed in terms of its ends, its costs, its benefits for the kind of social compact that exists in schools, and its impact on autonomy. Extreme order-keeping should be subject to the same remedies that apply to extreme teacher differences in style: principals, in cooperation with school boards, should establish what is not suitable and should monitor and enforce standards of reasonableness both for themselves and for teachers. In many schools, changes in order-keeping are achieved only through changes in top personnel. It may be that the principal does not need to interpret, monitor, and enforce; it may be better that the principal exit.

3.   Discrimination. The issues of discrimination raised in this study are very tangled and difficult ones. These schools are middle class in their curriculum and discriminate in their discipline system toward middle-class children. Many scholars contend that the role of schools in society has traditionally been one of talking democracy and implementing elitism. They argue that schools as part of the

general capitalist society sort people into elite and working class groups and that there is nothing unintentional about the fact that schools send different messages and offer different rewards to children of different backgrounds.[12] It is not our intention to engage in a confrontation with this literature. Rather, for the schools we have studied, we would suggest that our data should be helpful in their bringing to a higher level of consciousness the amount of middle-class bias in their system. Then the school staff (and community) can begin to grapple with the consequences of such orientation.

On a simple level, our data reveal that kids in school recognize discrimination even when it is of a fairly subtle sort. To teachers and administrators, this should suggest the need to be aware that disciplinary reactions may indeed be inappropriately colored by the whole role of the youth in school, and that kids are very sensitive to the lack of even-handedness. For teachers and staff, there are good reasons to be aware of the negative consequences of such labelling, since it is detected by children in school and considered to be evidence of different treatment. Since students have little use for unfair teachers, they will make life harder for them. The outcome of teacher discrimination in punishing others is, we suggest, that the teacher gets punished, too.

4. Troubled schools. For a severely troubled school it is useful to begin with identifying the general remedies that will not work. Demythification, in a school so centrally wedded to its myths, will not be effective. Thinking through, with the myths still present and central, will not be successful, nor will coordination. The sports model, getting a new coach, will not usually be successful because the structural and social ties of the organization were in themselves problems. "Within-school" remedy rules or approaches are much less likely to be successful with the troubled school than outside intervention. If new leadership means new structural and social arrangements, then the troubled school may overcome the limitations imposed by its myth. Certainly some outside influence, perhaps the "organizational doctor" or a community-citizen task force is needed to move the institution off center and induce it to stop punishing itself.

5. Junior high schools. Junior high schools and middle schools raise problems that educational philosophy has been least able to approach. The educational philosophy appropriate to junior highs should clearly not be the one applied to elementary school pupils. There is evidence that junior high pupils, while of mixed role and age orientation, incline much more toward high school responsible youth models than toward any other. We would suggest that junior

high schools give serious consideration to loosening up, to treating students as responsible youth, not older "children," and to exploring the development of choice models to a much greater extent.

European school systems traditionally have not age segregated youth into middle and junior high schools. Perhaps those experiences should be subjected to more careful study as American schools face enrollment declines that may cause changes in age groupings as well as geographical boundaries.[13]

6. Troubled students. It is our position that the appropriate educational response of schools is, first, to develop and apply a range of alternative within-school techniques to try to make the school environment meaningful to the student and, second, should those efforts fail to recognize that within-school techniques may finally just be wasting everyone's time, and to release the student into a carefully considered alternative setting.

Will schools want to adopt these approaches? If so, which ones? Institutional remedies can be measured on a variety of continua, the most important probably being their cost. Although remedies can be sorted as to the impact they will have on the problem presented, the amount of community tension engendered by their proposal, etc., most schools react to proposals for change primarily in terms of dollars and cents costs. There are also nonmonetary costs, even harder to quantify. Many institutions routinely conduct cost-benefit analyses in the process of making a choice among proposals. For schools these analyses are much harder to accomplish. How can one quantify a reduction in school suspensions of ten percent, or a change in the suspension dropout cycle? What is its dollar benefit? What is the benefit of reduced truancy, especially if the state does not use average daily attendance figures to determine financial reimbursement to the school district? How can one compare the benefit of dropout reduction to suspension reduction?

For some kinds of problems, benefits are direct and measurable. Vandalism costs money and its reduction may save dollars for the school which can be made available for other purposes, but for most problems the cost-benefit kind of analysis is more difficult. Cost-benefit analysis, therefore, usually cannot be used to assess the appeal of different remedies. Schools tend to fall back on other criteria.

Remedies that will be chosen are likely to have certain characteristics. The remedies or innovations that most school organizations will explore are those which are the lowest in cost and risk. These are unlikely to confront deep-seated problems with the structure of schooling or educational goals. For the most part they will be within-institution changes involving a minimum of outside actors and resources. The principal must endorse them and preferably champion them. There is a kind of Catch-22 in effect, in that the stronger and more confident a teaching and administrative staff, the more willing they will be to undertake substantial efforts with some risks (to involve community people, to work directly with students on an open-ended task force), whereas, the more troubled schools will venture less.

E. Conclusion

For the most part, our analysis of discipline and its roots in the structure and philosophy of the school have reinforced our expectation that the American educational system will continue in the future much as it has since the Second World War. We assume thus that alternative schools and programs will continue to exist, but that most school children will go to schools quite a bit like those their parents attended. Yet, as our study has shown, there is reason to be very concerned about this relatively static picture. Schools, with their indirect and direct middle-class biases are contributing to the further alienation of a minority of youth and are carrying out a pattern of unrecognized discrimination. Lacking good, systematic information about discipline patterns, schools fall prey to myths and stereotypes. Although myths and stereotypes afford a sense of security, they are often wrong-headed and can do serious disservice to the schools, their staffs, and their students.

How likely is it that schools will be active in their concern with such issues? There has been quite a bit of activity with reference to public secondary education in the 1960s and 1970s. Questions of decentralization, vouchers, and de-schooling have all been aired. The cadre of students and teachers associated with the Vietnam years brought to the schools perspectives that were fresh and often painful. Citizen education groups developed in several hundred communities and publications about open schooling were common. Federal and state money for program diversification and innovation were often available. Thus, for two decades a variety of forces stimulated a considerable amount of debate about schools.

The 1980s are clearly a time of enormous financial pressure on the public school system. The enrollment declines, to date felt most heavily in elementary schools, are appearing in secondary schools as well, so that management for decline in education has become a dominant note in

educational exchanges.[14] The demography of the teaching
profession is such that a very large number of middle-aged
teachers, protected by union contracts, are quite likely to
remain in the schools for the next thirty years, with few
new faces joining them. Some teachers will retire, burn out,
or enter administration, but by and large there will be little
new hiring for several years. The personnel now in place
will be the personnel called upon to increase alternatives,
coordinate plans, handle implicit discrimination--in short, to
address the types of problems we have discussed in schools.

It is not an auspicious time for American education.
School populations will probably continue to become more
heterogenous as the forces of societal mixing work
themselves out. More heterogeneous school populations,
requiring rethinking traditional ways, will be met by
ever-more-centralized management perspectives as budgeting
becomes the unchallenged key to education. The higher-cost
alternative schools, like magnet schools, will be threatened
because of per-pupil costs. The school personnel who will
be charged on a building level with decision making will be
increasingly distant in age from the students and may be
increasingly prone to retreat to what seems familiar rather
than risk censure for alternatives.

These are all reasons to be somewhat glum about the
ability of schools to solve many of their problems. There is
another side, to be considered however. From school after
school comes the report that more tranquil societal times of
the late 1970s and the stabilization of teaching staff have
facilitated grassroots efforts to identify and solve problems
before they get any worse. Schools, without the demands
placed on them by expansion, and eager to keep support in
times of enrollment decline and budget shortfalls, seem
somewhat willing to experiment with new age groupings,
personalization of education through small classes, etc.
They want to keep students in school, and to a certain
extent they are thinking in terms of tailoring their services
to suit the market. These micro, or building-level steps, if
diffused and shared, offer some possibility that the politics
of educational scarcity may generate a time of
self-examination and creative response. Finally, the spectre
of courts running schools, so vivid to some commentators in
1975, has faded. Schools have learned that they are able to
undertake quite complex systems for special education pupils
in a very short period of time. They have found themselves
able to incorporate the benefits of challenges ranging from
Sputnik to bilingualism, able to withstand considerable
unfamiliar stress. In the current mood of self-examination,
schools seem to be turning to the problem they have kept in
the closet: discipline. As they do so, they find as we have

that discipline is anything but a discrete, separable problem. To confront it will mean talking about the structure of schooling and educational goals. These are hard issues, hard both in that they are so pervasive and threatening and in that so little is known. For education, thus, the challenge of "discipline" is a mighty one. But schools seem to be beginning to recognize the clear ties that exist among order, autonomy, discipline, and learning. As part of their concerns with being more effective, schools--at least, some schools--have begun to be much more explicit about how their goals and their structures interact, and the implications of these parameters for school discipline.

NOTES

[1]"Review Symposium," American Educational Research Journal 15 (1978); B.S. Bloom, Human Characteristics and School Learning (New York: McGraw-Hill, 1976).

[2]See Richard Pratte, The Public School Movement: A Critical Study (New York: McKay, 1973).

[3]The study recently completed by Professor Wellford W. Wilms of UCLA suggests that vocational education in public school does not operate efficiently to improve earning prospects for students.

[4]Lucius F. Cervantes, The Dropout: Causes and Cures (Ann Arbor: University of Michigan Press, 1965), Chapter 3; National Council on Crime and Delinquency, Theoretical Perspectives on School Crime, (Springvield, Va.: National Technical Information Service, 1978) Sections I and II, Parts I, II, and III.

[5]Daniel L. Duke, "Who Misbehaves? A High School Studies Its Discipline Problems," Educational Administration Quarterly 12 (1976).

[6]Dan C. Lortie, Schoolteacher: A Sociological Study (Chicago: University of Chicago Press, 1975).

[7]Exploration of the complexities and interconnections of change is found in Richard C. Williams, Charles C. Wall, W. Michael Martin, and Arthur Berchin, Effecting Organizational Renewal in Schools: A Social Systems Perspective (New York: McGraw-Hill, 1974).

[8]Chris   Argyris,   Organization   and   Innovation
(Homewood,   Illinois: Dorsey,   1965);   Chris   Argyris,
"Theories of Action That Inhibit Learning," American
Psychologist 31 (1976).

[9]The complexities of defining disorder are explored in
Peter Marsh, Elizabeth Rosser, and Rom Harre, The Rules of
Disorder (London: Routledge and Kegan Paul, 1978).

[10] Daniel L. Duke, The Retransformation of the School
(Chicago: Nelson-Hall, 1978); Terrence E. Deal and Robert
R. Nolan, Alternative Schools: Ideologies, Realities, Guide-
lines (Chicago: Nelson-Hall, 1978).

[11]Mark G. Yudof, "Procedural Fairness and Substantive
Justice: Due   Process,   Bureaucracy,   and   the   Public
Schools," in June Newitt, ed., Future Trends in Education
Policy (Lexington, Mass: D.C. Heath, 1979).

[12]Delinquency Prevention: Theories   and   Strategies
(Washington: Office of Juvenile Justice and Delinquency
Prevention, 1979).

[13]Recent research on the grade groupings in which
seventh graders fare best suggests that the placement of
students may affect their behavior and thus the climate of
the school.

[14]Susan Abramovitz and Stuart Rosenfeld, eds., Declining Enrollment: The   Challenge   of   the   Coming   Decade
(Washington: National Institute of Education, 1978); "Declining School Enrollments" issue of Education and Urban
Society", 11 (1979).

BIBLIOGRAPHY

Books and Monographs

Abramovitz, Susan and Stuart Rosenfeld, eds., Declining Enrollment: The Challenge of the Coming Decade (Washington: National Institute of Education, 1978).

Alschuler, Alfred, School Discipline: A Socially Literate Solution (New York: McGraw-Hill Book Co., 1980).

Argyris, Chris, Organization and Innovation (Homewood, Ill: Dorsey, 1965).

Baur, Marilyn S., Truancy: An Examination of Social Structural Influences and Traditional Approaches (unpublished doctoral dissertation, Univ. of Colorado, Boulder, 1976).

Benoit, Richard P., "An Investigation of Eighth Grade Student Attitudes Regarding Middle School Disciplinary Practices" (unpublished doctoral dissertation, Florida Atlantic Univ., 1975).

Berger, Michael, Violence in the Schools: Causes and Remedies (Bloomington: Phi Delta Kappa Educational Foundation, 1974).

Bloom, B.S., Human Characteristics and School Learning (New York: McGraw-Hill, 1976).

Bolmeier, Edward C., Legality of Student Disciplinary Practices (Charlottesville, Va.: The Michie Co., 1976).

Bowles, Samuel and Herbert Gintis, Schooling in Capitalist America (New York: Basic Books, 1976).

Brookover, Wilbur, School Social Systems and Student Achievement (New York: Praeger, 1979).

Cervantes, Lucius F., The Dropout: Causes and Cures (Ann Arbor: University of Michigan Press, 1965).

Children's Defense Fund, Children Out of School in America
    (Washington: Washington   Research   Project,   Inc.,
    1974).

----------, School Suspensions (Washington: Washington Re-
    search Project, Inc., 1975).

Cicourel, Aaron V. and John I. Kitsuse, The Educational
    Decision-Makers   (Indianapolis: Bobbs-Merrill   Co.,
    1963).

Citizen's Council for Ohio Schools, Children Out of School in
    Ohio (Columbus, 1972).

Community Relations-Social Development Commission, Special
    Student Concerns Project: Phase I Research Report
    (Milwaukee County, Wis., 1978).

Deal, Terrence E. and Robert R. Nolan, Alternative Schools:
    Ideologies, Realities, Guidelines (Chicago: Nelson-Hall,
    1978).

DeCecco, John and Arlene Richards, Growing Pains--Uses of
    School Conflict (New York: Aberdeen Press, 1974).

Dolbeare, Kenneth and Paul Hammond, The School Prayer
    Decisions   (Chicago: University   of   Chicago   Press,
    1971).

Duke, Daniel L., The Retransformation of the School
    (Chicago: Nelson-Hall, 1978).

Duke, Daniel L., ed., Helping Teachers Manage Classrooms
    (Alexandria, Va.:   Association for Supervision and
    Curriculum Development, 1982).

Faust, Naomi, Discipline and the Classroom Teacher (Port
    Washington, N.Y.: Kennikat Press, 1977).

Friedman, Robert, Family Roots of School Learning and Be-
    havior Disorders (Springfield, Ill.:   Charles C.
    Thomas, 1973).

Galbraith, Ronald and Thomas Jones, Moral Reasoning: A
    Teaching Handbook for Adapting Kohlberg to the Class-
    room (Anoka, Minn.: Greenhave Press, 1976).

Goffman, Erving, Stigma (Englewood Cliffs, N.J.: Prentice-
    Hall, Inc., 1963).

Guskin, Alen E. and Samuel L. Guskin, A Social Psychology
    of Education (Reading, Mass.:   Addison-Wesley Publish-
    ing Co., 1970).

Hargreaves, David, Social Relations in a Secondary School
    (London: Routledge and Kegan Paul, 1967).

Jackson, Phillip, Life in Classrooms (New York: Holt,
    Rinehart and Winston, 1968).

Hollingshead, August B., Elmtown's Youth (New York: John
    Wiley, 1949).

Hollingsworth,   Ellen   Jane,   ed.,   "Discipline   in
    Schools--Roots, Rights and Remedies," 11 Education and
    Urban Society 4 (1979).

Jencks, Christopher, Marshall Smith, Henry Acland, Mary Jo
    Bane, David Cohen, Herbert Gintis, Barbara Heyns,
    and Stephen Michelson, Inequality (New York: Basic
    Books, 1972).

Kounin, J.S., Discipline and Group Management in Class-
    rooms (New York: Holt, Rinehart, Winston, 1970).

Lortie, Dan C., School Teacher: A Sociological Study
    (Chicago: University of Chicago Press, 1975).

Manchak, P. Susan and Steven R., The New Psychology of
    Classroom Discipline and Control (West Nyack, N.Y.:
    Parker Publishing Co., 1981).

Marsh, Peter, Elizabeth Rosser and Rom Harre, The Roles of
    Disorder (London: Routledge and Kegan Paul, 1978).

Maryland Association of Secondary School Principals, Final
    Report of the Task Force on Educational Programs for
    Disruptive Youth (Annapolis, Md.:   Maryland Depart-
    ment of Education, 1976).

Metz, Mary Haywood, Classrooms and Corridors (Berkeley:
    University of California Press, 1978).

National Council on Crime and Delinquency, Theoretical Per-
    spective on School Crime (Springfield, Va.:   National
    Technical Information Service, 1978).

National Institute of Education, Violent Schools--Safe Schools
    (Washington, D.C., 1977).

Office of Juvenile Justice and Delinquency Prevention, De-
    linquency   Prevention: Theories   and   Strategies
    (Washington: U.S. Government Printing Office, 1979).

Pratte, Richard, The Public School Movement: A Critical
    Study (New York: McKay, 1973).

Rich, John M., Discipline and Authority in School and Family
    (Lexington: Lexington Books, 1982).

Rosenbaum, James, Making Inequality: The Hidden Curric-
    ulum of High School Tracking (New York: John Wiley &
    Sons, 1976).

Reich, Charles A., The Greening of America (New York:
    Bantam Books, 1970).

Rutter, Michael, Fifteen Thousand Hours (Cambridge:
    Harvard University Press, 1979).

Sarason, Seymour, The Culture of the School and the Prob-
    lem of Change (Boston: Allyn and Bacon, 1973).

Schwartz, Bernard, Constitutional Law: A Textbook (New
    York: Macmillan, 2nd ed., 1979).

Schur, Edwin M., Labeling Deviant Behavior (New York:
    Harper & Row, 1971).

Sevick, Kevin J., Disruptive Student Behavior in the Class-
    room: What Research Says to the Teacher (Washington,
    D.C.: National Education Association, 1980).

Sharp, Rachel and Anthony Green, with Jacqueline Lewis,
    Education and Social Control (London: Routledge and
    Kegan Paul, 1975).

Shoham, Shlomo, The Mark of Cain: The Stigma Theory of
    Crime and Social Deviation (Dobbs Ferry, N.Y.: Oceana
    Publications, Inc., 1970).

Stinchcombe, Arthur, Rebellion in a High School (Chicago:
    Quadrangle, 1964).

Stoops, Emery and Joyce King-Stoops, Discipline or
    Disaster? (Bloomington: Phi Delta Kappa Educational
    Foundation, 1975).

Wayson, William W., Handbook for Developing Schools with Good Discipline (Bloomington: Phi Delta Kappa Educational Foundation, 1982).

Williams, Richard C., Charles C. Wall, W. Michael Martin and Arthur Berdin, Effecting Organizational Renewal in Schools: A Social System Perspective (New York: McGraw-Hill, 1974).

Willis, Paul, Learning to Labour: How Working Class Kids Get Working Class Jobs (Westmead, England: Sexon House, 1977).

Wisconsin Department of Public Instruction, Student Rights in Wisconsin Public Elementary and Secondary Schools (Madison, Wis.: September, 1977).

Wolfgang, Charles H. and Carl D. Glickman, Solving Discipline Problems: Strategies for Classroom Teachers (Boston: Allyn and Bacon, 1982).

Articles

Abrell, Ronald L., "Classroom Discipline Without Punishment," Clearinghouse 50 (December, 1976).

Apple, Michael W., "Common Sense Categories and Curriculum Thought," Schools in Search of Meaning, James B. MacDonald and Esther Zaret, eds. (Washington: Association for Supervision and Curriculum Development, 1975).

Apple, Michael W. and Nancy King, "What Do Schools Teach?" Curriculum Theory, Alex Molnar and John Zahorik, eds. (Washington: Association for Supervision and Curriculum Development, 1977).

Argryis, Chris, "Theories of Action That Inhibit Learning," American Psychologist 31 (1976).

Bennett, Christine and J. John Harris III, "Suspensions and Expulsions of Male and Black Students: A Study of the Causes of Disproportionality," Urban Education 16 (1982).

Bocciardi, Gerald, "Suspension: The Approach Positive," Journal of Secondary Education, 38 (1963).

Brown, Lorraine Hayes, Donald J. Willower and Patrick D. Lynch, "School Socioeconomic Status and Teacher Pupil Control Behavior," 9 Urban Education 3 (October, 1974).

Carlson, R. O., "Environmental Constraints and Organizational Consequences: The Public School and Its Clients," Behavioral Science and Educational Administration, D. E. Griffiths, ed. (Chicago: University of Chicago Press, 1969).

Center for New Schools, "Strengthening Alternative High Schools," Harvard Educational Review 42 (August, 1972).

Diprete, Thomas A., "Discipline and Order in an American High School," Report of National Opinion Research Center (Chicago, November, 1981).

Doyle, Walter, "Helping Teachers Manage Classrooms," NAASP Bulletin 59 (December, 1975).

Duke, Daniel, "Who Misbehaves--A High School Studies Its Discipline Problems," 12 Educational Administration Quarterly 3 (1976).

Duke, Daniel and Cheryl Terry, "What Happened to the High School Discipline Crisis?" Urban Education 14 (1979).

Duncan, Otis D., "A Socioeconomic Index for all Occupations," Occupation and Social Status, Albert Reiss, Jr., ed. (New York: Free Press, 1961).

Feldhusen, J.F., "A Longitudinal Study of the Correlates of Children's Social Behavior," (Bethesda, Md: ERIC Document ED079634, 1973).

Goldstein, Burton, Jr., "Due Process in the Public Schools," North Carolina Law Review 54 (1976).

Grantham, Marvin L. and Clifton S. Harris Jr., "A Faculty Trains Itself to Improve Student Discipline," Phi Delta Kappan 57 (June, 1976).

Greenberger, David B., "An Aesthetic Theory of School Vandalism," 24 Crime and Delinquency 3 (July, 1978).

Guttmann, Joseph, "Pupils', Teachers' and Parents' Causal Attributions for Problem Behavior at School," 76 Journal of Educational Research 1 (1982).

Haney, Walt and George Madaus, "Making Sense of the Competency Testing Movement," 48 Harvard Educational Review 4 (November, 1978).

Harris, Karen, Glennelle Halpin and Gerald Halpin, "Personality Characteristics and Self Concept of Preservice Teachers Related to Their Pupil Control Orientation," 50 Journal of Experimental Education 21 (1982).

Hollingsworth, Ellen Jane, "Fairness and Discretion: Exemptions in Wisconsin," Report to the National Institute of Education, (Madison: Center for Public Representation, January, 1981).

---------, "The Impact of Student Rights and Discipline Cases on Schools," Schools and the Courts, Vol. 2 (Eugene, Or.: Clearinghouse on Educational Management, 1979).

Howard, Eugene R., "School Discipline--Helping the Teacher: Improving Discipline by Improving the School," (Reston, Va.: National Association of Secondary School Principals, 1982).

Jensen, Gary J. and Raymond Eve, "Sex Differences in Delinquency," Criminology 13 (1976).

Kaestle, Carl F., "Social Change, Discipline, and the Common School in Early 19th Century America," 9 Journal of Interdisciplinary History 1 (Summer, 1978).

Kendall, Arthur J., "Teachers' Perceptions of and Reactions to Misbehavior in Traditional and Open Classrooms," 67 Journal of Educational Psychology 4 (1975).

Kirp, David, "Proceduralism and Bureaucracy: Due Process in the School Setting," 28 Stanford Law Review 841 (1976).

Kohlberg, Lawrence, "Stage and Sequence: The Cognitive-Developmental Approach to Socialization," Handbook of Socialization Theory and Research, D. Gaslin ed. (Chicago: Rand McNally, 1969).

----------, "From Is to Ought...," Cognitive Development and Epistemology, T. Mischel, ed. (New York: Academic Press, 1971).

Kohlberg, Lawrence and Rochelle Mayer, "Development as the Aim of Education," 42 Harvard Educational Review 2 (1972).

Lazerson, Marvin, "Revisionism and American Educational History," 43 Harvard Educational Review 2 (1973).

Lines, Patricia, "The Case Against Short Suspensions," 12 Inequality in Education 41 (July, 1972).

Lockhart, W., Yale Kamisar and J. Choper, "Four Decades of Judicial Abstention," The American Constitution: Cases and Materials (St. Paul: West, 1981).

Lufler, Henry S., Jr., "Discipline: A New Look at an Old Problem," 59 Phi Delta Kappan 6 (1978).

Manley-Casimir, Michael E., "School Governance as Discretionary Justice," School Review 82 (1974).

Mashaw, Jerry, "Conflict and Compromise Among Models of Administrative Justice," 1981 Duke Law Journal 2 (1981).

----------, "Administrative Due Process: The Quest for a Dignitary Theory," Boston University Law Review 61 (July, 1981).

McNeil, Linda, "Student Rights and the Social Context of Schooling," Schooling and the Rights of Children, Vernon Haubrich and Michael Apple, eds. (Berkeley: McCutchan Publishing Corp., 1975).

Miles, Matthew B., "Mapping the Common Properties of Schools," Improving Schools: Using What We Know, Rolf Lehming and Michael Kane, eds. (Beverly Hills: Sage Publications, 1981).

Medway, Frederic J., "Causal Attributions for School-Related Problems: Teacher Perceptions and Teacher Feedback," 71 Journal of Educational Psychology 6 (1979).

Olneck, Michael R. and David B. Bills, "What Makes Sammy Run? An Empirical Assessment of the Bowles-Gintis

Correspondence Theory," American Journal of Education (November, 1980).

Purkey, Stewart C. and Marshall S. Smith, "Effective Schools: A Review," Elementary School Journal 427 (March, 1983).

Rank, Allan D., "Conflict in the Classroom," Conflict Resolution Through Communication, Fred E. Jandt, ed. (New York: Harper & Row, 1973).

Redl, Fritz, "Disruptive Behavior in the Classroom," 80 School Review 569 (August, 1975).

Rosenfeld, Gerry, "Shut Those Thick Lips! Can't You Behave Like a Human Being?" Schooling in the Cultural Context, Joan I. Roberts and Sherie K. Akinsanya, eds. (New York: David McKay Co., Inc., 1976).

Rutter, Michael, "School Effects on Pupil Progress: Research Findings and Policy Implications," Handbook of Teaching and Policy, Lee S. Shulman and Gary Sykes, eds. (New York: Longman Press, 1983).

Sørensen, Aage Bottger, "Organizational Differentiation of Students and Education Opportunity," 42 Sociology of Education 355 (Fall, 1970).

Stretch, John and Phillip Crunk, "School Suspension: Help or Hindrance?" The School in the Community, Rosemary Sari and Frank E. Maple, eds. (Washington: National Association of Social Workers, Inc., 1972).

Tractenberg, Paul, "Testing for Minimum Competency: A Legal Analysis," Minimum Competency Achievement Testing, Richard M. Jaeger and Carol Tittle, eds. (Berkeley: McCutchan Publishing, 1980).

Tumin, Melvin, "Schools as Social Organizations," Perspectives on Organizations: The Schools as a Social Organization, Roger Corwin, R. A. Edelfelt, T. E. Andrews, and B. L. Bryan, eds. (Washington: American Association of Colleges for Teacher Education and Association of Teacher Educators, 1977).

West, W. Gordon, "Adolescent Deviance and the School," 6 Interchange 2 (1975).

Werthamm, Carl, "Delinquents in Schools: A Test for the Legitimacy of Authority," Berkeley Journal of Sociology 8 (1963).

Wittig, Monika, "Client Control and Organizational Dominance: The School, Its Students and Their Parents," Social Problems 24 (1976).

Yudof, Mark, "Suspension and Expulsion of Black Students from the Public Schools: Academic Capital Punishment and the Constitution," 39 Law and Contemporary Problems 2 (Spring, 1975).

---------, "Liability for Constitutional Torts and the Risk-Adverse Public School Official," Southern California Law Review 49 (September, 1976).

---------, "Procedural Fairness and Substantive Justice: Due Process, Bureaucracy and the Public Schools," Future Trends in Education Policy, Jane Newitt, ed. (Lexington: D.C. Heath, 1979).

---------, "Legalization of Dispute Resolution, Distrust of Authority, and Organizational Theory: Implementing Due Process for Students in the Public Schools," University of Wisconsin Law Review (1981).

Discussion Papers and Notes

Hermanson, Don, "School Discipline--What the Discipline Records Tell Us," (Madison: Center for Public Representation, Staff Paper, March, 1977).

Kirp, David L., "The Fourth R: Reading, Writing, 'Rithmetic--and Rules," Policy Paper No. 83-C1, Institute for Research on Educational Finance and Governance, Stanford University (February, 1983).

Maslach, Christine, "Burnout: A Social Psychological Analysis," paper presented to the American Psychological Association, August, 1977.

McPartland, James M. and Edward L. McDill, "The Unique Role of Schools in the Causes of Youthful Crime," Report 216, Center for Social Organization of Schools, Johns Hopkins University (1976).

Note: "The Pain of Teacher Burnout: A Case History," Phi
    Delta Kappan 61 (December, 1979).

Purkey, Stewart C. and Marshall S. Smith, "Ends Not
    Means, The Policy Implications of Effective Schools Re-
    search," (Madison: Wisconsin Center for Education
    Research, Working Paper, August, 1982).

Strunk, William, "Exclusion from School as a Disciplinary
    Tool" (Washington: National Association of Secondary
    School Principals, 1969).

"Student Wrongs Versus Student Rights," Nation's Schools
    and Colleges (April, 1975).

ABOUT THE AUTHORS

ELLEN JANE HOLLINGSWORTH has been Research Director of the Center for Public Representation and Project Associate at the Institute for Research on Poverty at the University of Wisconsin-Madison. She is the author (with Handler) of The Deserving Poor (Chicago: Markham, 1971), (with Handler and Erlanger) of Lawyers and the Pursuit of Legal Rights (New York: Academic Press, 1978), and (with R. Hollingsworth) of Dimensions of American Cities: Toward the Integration of History and Social Science (Madison: University of Wisconsin Press, 1979). Her ongoing research is concerned with educational organizations, hospital performance, and mental health community programs. She has assisted school administrators in the implementation of school discipline research findings.

HENRY S. LUFLER, JR., is Assistant Dean of the School of Education at the University of Wisconsin-Madison and was Project Director of the School Discipline Research Project at the Center for Public Representation. He edited (with Apple and Subkoviak) Educational Evaluation: Analysis and Responsibility (Berkeley: McCutchan Publishing Corp., 1974) and has written articles on educational research, the impact of legal institutions on schools, and the politics of education. He writes the "Pupils" chapter for the annual Yearbook of School Law, published by the National Organization on Legal Problems of Education. He was a member of Phi Delta Kappa's National Commission studying the impact of courts on schools.

WILLIAM H. CLUNE III is Professor at the University of Wisconsin Law School where he teaches education law, constitutional law, insurance law, and various courses in law and social science. He is also a faculty associate of the Wisconsin Center for Education Research where he is working on the problem of excessive "legalism" in government policy in education. He has written several articles on school finance and was the author (with Coons and Sugarman) of Private Wealth and Public Education (Cambridge: Harvard University Press, 1970). Recently, under grants from the

National Institute of Education, he has written on the implementation of legal policy in education, a paper on the "Deregulation Critique of the Federal Role in Education," and two long articles attempting to define and illustrate the scope and contents of "implementation" as a field of practical and research expertise.